WORK IT!

GET IN, GET NOTICED, GET PROMOTED

D0109584

DENISE M. DUDLEY

Published by SkillPath® Publications

Denise's royalties from the sale of *Work It!* will be donated to educational youth programs throughout the world.

Library of Congress Control Number: 2017940336

ISBN: 978-1-60811-738-3

Printed in the United States of America

MORE PRAISE FOR DENISE DUDLEY'S *WORK IT!*

"Denise's book addresses the last mile that exists between completing a degree or certification and finding the right first job toward a fulfilling career. The ROI on the thousands of dollars required to complete technical training or a degree depends on addressing these core elements to career success, for which the vast majority of students are largely uncertain and highly anxious. *Work It!* should be required reading for all sophomores and juniors at both the high school and college level."

—Scott Dawson, Dean, Orfalea College of Business, Cal Poly

"Denise's book, *Work It!*, is a valuable tool for young adults entering the working world. She provides useful information that will not only enhance the reader's communication skills, but also build his or her confidence. We look forward to sharing this book with our club members, and we also look forward to bringing Denise back as a guest speaker this year—our students really enjoy her talks!"

—Patricia Siqueiros, Executive Director, Variety Boys & Girls Club

"As the founder and CEO of The Literacy Company, which connects very personally with young people all over the world on an everyday basis, I believe that Denise's new book, *Work It!*, is an extremely valuable resource for anyone who's looking to find his or her right place in the working world. It's packed with such detailed, practical information that's actually useable! And it's written in a very friendly, readable style. I look forward to sharing this book with all the young people in my life."

—Richard Sutz, Founder and CEO, The Literacy Company;
Author, *Speed Reading for Dummies*

"As the CEO of a movie theatre corporation whose staff is comprised almost exclusively of persons under the age of 30, we serve as a first-time employer for many bright, exceptional young people entering the workforce. As such, Galaxy Theatres functions as a stepping stone for many who are looking to find their path to a fulfilling career, whether within the company or beyond—and I believe we have an obligation to help our people find their path. Denise's book is a valuable, insightful, truthful resource for anyone looking to find their optimal place in the working world. I wish it had been available when I started my career. I intend to recommend *Work It!* to all of our employees, supervisors, and managers in our theatres across the country."

—Frank J. Rimkus, CEO, Galaxy Theatres, LLC

"It's about time that someone wrote a book that truly helps young people with strategies for choosing and navigating the challenges of career choices! Denise's new book, *Work It!*, is targeted at the young people of today, whether they are just starting out in their careers, or are considering a career change, and are looking for guidance that's geared specifically toward their values, interests, and experiences. Through working with young people across the U.S. for many years, Denise has pinpointed the most important information needed, and she delivers it in a friendly, 'arm-chair chat' style that's easy to read. This is definitely a must-read for anyone who's interested in personal success."

—Lawrence J. Cohen, PharmD, BCPP, FASHP, FCCP, Professor of Pharmacotherapy, Coordinator of Interprofessional Education, and Coordinator of Continuing Professional Education, University of North Texas, System College of Pharmacy

"As both the father of a college senior, and as President of a bank that employs thousands of people, I must say that Denise's newest book, *Work It!*, is target-specific reading for anyone looking to get hired, get noticed, and get promoted. Easy to read, nicely organized, and to-the-point without being 'preachy,' I will definitely recommend this book to every young person I know."

—Kevin Barth, President, Commerce Bank

"As the Vice President of Brand Marketing for the world's largest global market research organization, I have the opportunity to work with countless young adults who are just starting out in their careers. Denise's newest book, *Work It!*, hits the nail on the head. She not only manages to share her wisdom in a friendly, helpful, useable format, but she also manages to make us laugh along the way and to remind us of our value as unique human beings. I believe that every young person will benefit from reading this book before starting out on a career path—in any field."

—Chris King, Vice President of Brand Marketing, J.D. Power

Did you ever pick up a book, open the cover, and wish it were dedicated to *you*? But, of course, it wasn't. How could it be, since the author doesn't even know you? Well, guess what? If you're reading this, then you're the person I'm dedicating my book to! But you're going to have to go ahead and read the whole thing for it to count—it's only fair. Thank you for inspiring me to write it, which you've done by being here to read it after it was written. (Whoa! This is sort of like one of those time warp sci-fi thingies.)

ACKNOWLEDGEMENTS

I'm relatively certain no one ever reads the acknowledgments page of any book. But I'm also equally sure that every book ever written should have an acknowledgements page about a mile long. Just like no person is an island, no book can possibly be written and published without the monumental help of others, and I'm so fortunate to have worked on this project with so many smart, talented, committed colleagues.

First of all, I want to thank Nadine Taylor, my wonderful editor and contributor, who spent countless hours making my random thoughts and scribbles eminently more readable than they otherwise would have been. She also cracked the whip and kept me on track with my deadlines. (Thanks, Nadine. You are truly the best in the biz.)

Secondly, thanks to Kristen Jones, Elizabeth Carter, and Emily Iorg for being the most outstanding proofreaders and commentators on the planet. Not only did they fix every typo and run-on sentence, but they also let me know what parts needed a rewrite, which I have hopefully fixed to their satisfaction. (Thanks, you three. You completely rock.)

Next, a giant shout-out goes to my own two children, Grant and Seth, plus a whole passel of my students, both past and present, for looking over my manuscript and making content suggestions, voting on which book cover design they liked best, and giving me pointers on how *not* to sound like a tedious academic. (Thanks, everyone, for helping me stay on the hip and groovy side of life. Peace out, muh babes.)

And next, my sincerest thanks go to Chad Pio, SkillPath's intrepid Director of Production and Marketing Media, and Julie Meloan, layout artist extraordinaire. They played around with several book titles and cover designs and lots of concepts for the inside format and layout, and after much consideration and effort, they finally came up with what you're holding in your hands. Pretty darn impressive, don't you think? (Thanks, Chad and Julie, for going the extra mile to create such a beautiful, readable book.)

Penultimately (such a fun word!), many thanks go to Matt Rhodes, Director of Publications, and Blanca Cuevas and Karen Kowalski, Lead Product Specialists, who run SkillPath's publication division, for publishing my book and for helping to make it available to young readers everywhere. (Thanks, you three. You really know your stuff in the publishing world, and it shows.)

And finally, I want to thank my entire SkillPath family of staff and faculty. I am honored to be associated with them, and I'm so proud to have founded a company that has brought so much good to the world. Through our 28-year journey together, I have learned and grown in ways I never could have imagined. (You are the finest group of people I have ever worked with, and I look forward to many more successful, fun-filled, productive years together. Party on, gang! I love you all.)

Once more, thank you to everyone for all your help. I absolutely couldn't have done it without every single one of you. What a phenomenal team!

TABLE OF CONTENTS

FOREWORD

This is what you'll learn in every writing class, including those I used to teach: Always write your opening last, after you've finished everything else. So here I am, having read, reread, re-re-read, revised, rewritten, changed, altered, refined, tweaked, and otherwise modified this entire book—the one that you're about to read. And now that I'm finished, I have a few observations ...

First of all, I've come to understand that I've been writing this book for much of my career, through all my seminars, keynotes, lectures, and curriculum development—it's simply taken me until recently to finally put pen to paper (or fingers to keyboard, in this case). This book holds much of my life's work. It contains many of the principles that I believe in. It's who I am and how I live my life. It's *me*, in a sense, in book form. I am very clearly a "how-to" kind of person, and I prefer concrete solutions and clear-cut answers over theories, conjecture, or speculation. In short, I'm a huge fan of practical application—and that's pretty much what you're going to find in the following pages.

Secondly, you've probably heard about "listicles" and the question-able press they've been receiving lately. You know, those slapdash, sometimes irritating articles that appear in certain magazines, where the writer somehow didn't have time to actually write something meaningful, so he simply pieced together a bunch of random ideas, numbered them one through ten, and then called it a day. But before you condemn listicles altogether, here's the thing: Lists can actually serve as an excellent format for organizing our thoughts, facilitating the learning process, and making complex topics more understandable and accessible. I teach in lists, I write in lists (as you're about to see), and I even *think* in lists. I am an unapologetic list person, because I believe *lists work*. So you guessed it: Get ready to read a book that contains quite a few (hopefully helpful) lists.

And lastly, in looking back on it all, I realize that I was inspired to write this book because of my genuine love for young people who are embarking on their life's journeys and careers. I wanted to write something that might help you on the road to happiness, success, and fulfillment. (Plus, I could literally find no book already written that targets your specific group and addresses the initial steps toward finding meaningful, rewarding employment.) I have the frequent pleasure of working with young people at various colleges, universities, high schools, clubs, and youth organizations, and I am constantly motivated by your electrifying enthusiasm and energy. You hold the future of this world in your hands, and I thoroughly trust you with its safekeeping. You are our next generation of change-makers, and it's an honor to spend a book's worth of time with you. Thank you for giving me this opportunity.

INTRODUCTION

Hello there, and welcome! I've been sitting here trying to imagine who you are and what you'd like to hear from me, and I've conjured up an image of you. You're most likely in your twenties or slightly younger, still in school or newly graduated. Or you might be a bit older and just beginning a new career path. You'd like to take charge of your work life, find a meaningful job, move up the ladder, secure an interesting and challenging position with lots of room for growth, earn a decent paycheck, and have a fun and fulfilling life. (And you're wondering where they're issuing the superhero underwear!)

Hey, I can definitely relate. Although I'm no longer a twentysomething (or even a fortysomething), there have been many times in my life when I've felt a lot like the way you might be feeling now. And, like you, one of my major goals (still) is to enjoy a fun and fulfilling life every single day. The biggest difference between you and me is that I've already done many of the things you want to do and learned a lot of lessons along the way. And I'd love nothing more than to share some of my knowledge and help you along on your journey.

My résumé is, well, varied, you might say. I began my work life selling snow cones in a ballpark, working for my parents in our family jewelry store, teaching swimming, serving as a lifeguard, selling lamps in a furniture store, and making sandwiches in a natural food store. And, at one glorious point along the way, I was actually a night-shift waitress at a truck stop! There was also a time when I was a fairly serious violinist—I even opted for a music major when I started college, and I spent my freshman year playing in the Sacramento Symphony, in California's state capital. But then I took my very first introductory psych course, fell in love with it, and decided I had found my passion. I eventually earned a PhD in behavioral psychology and did my postdoctoral work in agoraphobia, becoming part of a team that developed the go-to method used to treat agoraphobia and several other related phobias to this very day. Along the way, I served as a grief counselor (don't ask me what a happy-go-lucky 23-year-old girl like me knew about grief) and a "field therapist" for housebound people suffering from agoraphobia.

Then, while I was still in graduate school, I took a job at Crestwood Hospital, where I started at the very bottom as a psychiatric aide. Early on, I began to rise through the ranks at Crestwood, becoming a staff trainer and, eventually, the clinical director of the entire corporation of 18 hospitals, a post I held for approximately 10 years. I loved Crestwood! I loved my job, the staff, the patients, and my boss (the owner of the company), Jim, who was always a pleasure to work with. While at Crestwood, I also taught at several state hospitals throughout California (I loved psychiatric work so much, I actually taught classes on my days off from my "regular job"—talk about loving my work!).

In addition, I became a featured speaker for several health care organizations, including the American Psychiatric Association and the California Association of Health Facilities, and gave talks to audiences as large as 1,200 people about communication, supervision, leadership, patient care, and how to talk to the press. I truly had zero complaints: I was well-paid, supported by those around me, and doing things I loved. But what I really wanted (you had to know *that* was coming) was to become a professional speaker. This probably sounds a little dramatic or irrational (or both)—stopping short in the middle of my mental health career, making a U-turn, and racing off in a completely unrelated direction. However, I'd given plenty of speeches and countless training seminars during my years at Crestwood, and I'd never felt more happy and comfortable than when standing in front of a group of people, telling them things I thought might help them. So after much soul-searching, I decided to give it all up—to leave what was definitely a dream job—and become a professional speaker with a company called National Seminars. It sounds crazy, I know. But I did it anyway and was soon touring the country giving seminars on professional image and communication skills, business writing, management skills, and (my favorite) personal relationships. In due course, I sold my home in California and moved to Kansas City, where National was headquartered, to accept the internal position of vice president of faculty, curricula, and publications. It was there that I met Jerry Brown, National's president, and my future business partner (*and* future husband).

Eventually, Jerry and I left National together and started our own seminar company, SkillPath Seminars. It's a very long story with several twists and turns (and more than a few challenges), but the gist of it is Jerry and I started SkillPath in my basement with nothing more than a phone, a couple of plastic chairs, and a table. And then we grew it into the world's largest public seminar company. In 1995, SkillPath was listed at 32 on the Inc. 500 (*Inc.* magazine's list of the fastest-growing companies in the U.S.). Within 10 years of its inception, SkillPath had become a major force in both the training industry and the business-related publishing industry, with 350 full-time employees, 700 trainers, and a gross revenue of $200 million. To date, SkillPath has trained more than 12 million people in the U.S., Canada, the U.K., Australia, New Zealand, and South Africa and was chosen by Microsoft® to be the primary public seminar training company to introduce its new products and updates. Can you tell that I'm proud of it? You're darn right I'm proud.

Jerry and I went on to have two wonderful sons, Grant and Seth, whom I adore, and we sold SkillPath to a university in 2000. I feel that I must tell you the extremely sad part of this story: Jerry was killed in a helicopter accident just two years later. I lost my husband, father of my children, business partner, and best friend. I spent the next several years journeying through the very darkest part of my life with my two young children, learning countless lessons about love, patience, personal resilience, and the power of positive thinking.

Although I no longer own SkillPath, I have maintained a close relationship with the company, serving as a consultant and advisor and sitting on its board of directors. And very recently, SkillPath purchased one of its competitors, National Seminars (yes, the company I left to found SkillPath), a move that temporarily brought me back into the company to assist in the integration process.

I currently make my living as a writer, business consultant, and professional speaker in the areas of management, communication, professional image, leadership, business growth, and direct marketing. I have no idea how many people I've addressed during my speaking career, but by now it must be in the hundreds of thousands—and it remains my very favorite thing to do. I also work extensively with young people (high school and college age), teaching them job interview, social, and communication skills and the basics of entrepreneurship. As I mentioned in the foreword, this part of my current career has been so much fun and so fulfilling that I was inspired to write this book!

So there you have it—my life and career in a nutshell. From what I do for a living, to what I do for fun, to my relationships with colleagues, friends, and family, I truly *love* my life. People sometimes ask me whether I'm privy to some fabulous secret that will change their lives. Of course, I don't have any such secret. However, I *do* have plenty of ideas about how to adopt a winning attitude, give yourself an edge, stand out in a crowd, and function more effectively at work, in relationships, and in life. My goal is to convey these ideas to you as simply and clearly as I can.

But here's the deal: Don't try to do *everything* I suggest, or you'll drive yourself crazy! Just browse through my suggestions and look for those that resonate with you. Then try practicing just one or two for, say, 30 days to see if you notice any positive changes in your relationships, the way you feel about yourself, and your life in general. I am completely convinced that you will, although these changes may be small at first. But little changes become bigger ones over time. And before you know it, you will find yourself on a path to greater success, happiness, and fulfillment than you ever imagined.

Wishing you all the best on your journey!

CHAPTER ONE
SET SOME GOALS AND GET MOVING

O kay. Whadaya say we get the bad news out of the way so we can focus on the positives for the rest of this book. The first thing I want to tell you, right off the bat, is that you're going to face some hard times during your career. There may be periods when it seems like the entire world is conspiring against you, and you'll feel like running off to French Polynesia to lie in the sun and eat breadfruit for the rest of your days. Unfair things will happen. At times, you may even start to lose hope. So for all those times when you find yourself at the end of your rope, here's a little hard-earned advice: Take a break if you can, try to detach from the problem and get some perspective on the matter, and realize that you won't know the outcome until time (maybe plenty of time) has passed. Allow me to share with you one of my favorite maxims, which has proven true over and over again throughout my life: *Sometimes you can't tell the bad news from the good, especially when you're stuck in the middle of it.* So keep your eye on your goals and don't give up on your dreams, no matter what the circumstances.

That little saying comes from direct personal experience. This is the essence of what happened: Within six months of my moving across the country to take the inside job at National, Jerry Brown, several other staff members, and I were forced out of the company for political reasons. It was the worst time of my professional life. I lost sleep; I couldn't eat; I was exhausted and unsure of my future. I found myself living in a tiny apartment, unemployed, far from friends and family, in a city I knew very little about, with no particular prospects for quickly rounding up another job.

However, my "bad news" was about to morph into one of the best things that ever happened to me. Since both of us were out of a job, Jerry and I made the decision to form our own seminar company, and we jumped right on our new goal. We named it SkillPath, and together, we set about creating what we believed would become the ideal company for all involved—for our employees, our clients, and ourselves. We worked extremely hard, put every penny we owned into the company, and loved every minute of it. Eventually, SkillPath grew to become the largest seminar company in the world—and it still is. Talk about serendipity! And I know for a fact that my life would not be as wonderful as it is today if I hadn't been forced to step out on a limb and forge a new future for myself. Being ousted from National was what freed Jerry and me to create SkillPath Seminars!

And so, you may be going through absolute despair, the driest of dry spells, or the losing streak to end all losing streaks. Lost that job? Passed over for the promotion? Broken up with your soul mate? Been outbid on the house you had your heart set on? You truly won't know whether this "disaster" is bad or good until you've gained some time and perspective and can determine what happens *next*. Then, just like my exit from National Seminars, you just might find out it was the best thing that could have happened to you. And that's why *goal setting* is vital to your success—you'll have something positive to aim for when times become tough and you're looking to discover the silver lining among the storm clouds.

Goal Setting—the Jumping-off Point

In the same way that a company or a corporation needs a well-thought-out business plan that contains viable growth strategies and metrics, you and your career need a plan. If you want to learn, grow, and succeed, you will need to define your goals and develop a reasonable strategy for accomplishing them.

The continual setting and achieving of goals is the foundation of a satisfying career—or, quite often, it's the continual setting and *modifying* of goals before they can be achieved. (And, while we're on the subject, goal setting is also the foundation of a satisfying *life*.) Of course, there are some people who have enjoyed glorious careers that seem to have dropped into their laps. We've all heard about Natalie Portman being discovered by a Revlon cosmetics agent in a pizzeria on Long Island and—just like that!—she became a star. Hugh Hefner's daughter, Christie, became the CEO of Playboy, Inc., and probably *not* because she worked her way up from the mailroom. And Steve Forbes, editor-in-chief of *Forbes* magazine and CEO of Forbes Publishing Company, inherited the job from his father, Malcom Forbes, who inherited it from *his* father, B. C. Forbes. Sometimes, being in the right place—or the right family—at the right time pays off.

For the rest of us, though, setting goals is absolutely crucial: In order to get somewhere, you must choose a direction. And then you must start moving toward it. (Many years ago, I wrote one of SkillPath's registered taglines: "Pick a Direction and Grow." That's how much I believe in goal setting—enough to put it on the cover of our company catalogs.)

But not just any old goal will do. Certain goals can sap your confidence, make you feel like a failure, and carry you off in the wrong direction. Still others can leave you spinning your wheels, getting nowhere. But some goals—the right goals—will spur you on to success. Like a beacon in the night, they'll continually lead you down the right path, as long as you keep focusing on them.

Goals that work for you

So how do you set goals that help rather than hinder? There are five essential parts to a worthy goal. It should be:

- **Reasonable:** "One day you can be president of the United States if you really want to," they told us when we were kids. And they insisted we should always "aim for the stars." Sky-high career goals may be inspiring for some, but they can be self-defeating for the majority of people. (Let's face it: Only one person at a time gets to be president, which leaves the rest of us out of a job!) That's because impossible or nearly impossible goals practically ensure you'll feel like a failure if or when you don't achieve them. And when that happens, you may just want to pick up your ball and go home. To avoid the "impossible goal syndrome," break down your long-term goals (e.g., getting into management) into something more realistic. Set smaller, bite-sized, daily goals, like showing up for work on time, spending at least 15 minutes networking with people who can help you, and getting all the way through a reasonable to-do list. These repeated successes will build your feelings of personal fulfillment *and* your confidence, while steadily moving you closer to your larger, long-term goals.

- **Specific:** Set clear-cut, simple goals. Instead of saying something vague like, "I want to move up the career ladder," say, "I'll get a degree in my field," or "I'll make sure that all my reports are on time and accurate." Once you've pinpointed some goals (no more than five at a time), write them down and say them out loud. Committing them to paper will make them more concrete. By thinking about them, saying them out loud, *and* writing them down, your brain will build multiple strong connections to your goals, making you more likely to be successful!

■ **Measurable:** This goes hand in hand with being specific. Make sure your goals have clear outcomes that you can see or quantify in some way. Instead of saying, "I'm going to be a better employee," say, "I will contribute at least one constructive idea to every staff meeting." This will make it easier for you to track your results. Either you reached your goal or you didn't.

■ **Adjustable:** If your goal is too rigid or impractical, it might not be attainable. For example, let's say you've set a goal of getting your master's degree no later than one year from today. But if you are working full-time, have two small children, and have suddenly found out you must vacate your house and move across town, your timeline for getting that degree will probably need to be lengthened. Or you may decide that it isn't really necessary, or maybe it's not something you truly want to do. Goals require not only ability and drive, but commitment and opportunity. Reevaluate each goal periodically and decide if it's still something you really want to pursue. Then give yourself the opportunity to change your mind or create more realistic or desirable goals. (Case in point: About 10 years ago, I changed my mind about wanting to learn to skydive. Jumping out of an airplane and hoping the parachute opens? What was I *thinking?* Sorry, avid skydivers—maybe I'm just a chicken!)

■ **Given a time frame:** Setting a deadline is particularly important, especially if you tend to procrastinate. Without a deadline, it may be hard to find a reason to act right *now;* there's no real sense of urgency. So pick an end date for achieving your goal (again, write it down), as in, "I'm going to make 10 cold calls before noon every day for one month."

On the end date, evaluate. Did you reach your goal? If so, pat yourself on the back. If not, ask yourself if you may have set your goal too high. Was it too complicated? Did you work hard enough at it? Was it something you really wanted to achieve? You may find that your goal needs to be tweaked, changed, or even possibly abandoned.

Make sure all of your career goals are reasonable, specific, measurable, adjustable, and given a time frame. And when they seem obsolete or they no longer work for you, get rid of them and set new ones!

Setting goals for our dream company

When Jerry and I started SkillPath back in April 1989, we set some very clear, attainable goals that we kept foremost in our minds throughout the life of the company. On our first day in the office, I kicked off my shoes, grabbed a marker, and because we had no furniture yet, set a little flip chart on the floor and got down on my knees in front of it. (I have an old photo taken that day by Jerry that proves it. I look like I'm wearing my pajamas, which we called a "pants suit" back then!) Jerry and I brainstormed, and using my marker, I wrote out the six goals that would form the ideology for our company. They were simple and clear:

- ■ **Be top dog:** We decided from the get-go that we wanted to dominate the seminar world; to be not only the best, but also the biggest. We were not aiming toward being a mom-and-pop organization. This may sound like one of those sky-high goals that I warned you about. But between the two of us, we had a great deal of knowledge about the seminar business, and I'd also gained plenty of experience in managing people during my former career at Crestwood. So becoming "the biggest and best" really wasn't a crazy goal for us. Instead, it motivated us from the very moment we founded the company, giving us the energy we needed to work long hours (for no pay in the beginning) and helping us stay focused. Naturally, we needed to break down our "top dog" goal into smaller, more manageable pieces—the first of which was to get some furniture!

- **Have fun:** This was the second goal we came up with, which tells me we were pretty darned serious about having fun! We were both firmly committed to the idea that if building and running a seminar company wasn't fun, then we weren't going do it: We would simply stop and go do something else. (We both had other careers that we could resume if we needed to—I, in the mental health world, and Jerry, in advertising.) Fortunately, we did have fun and became successful almost immediately, so we never had to throw in the towel. In fact, I can truthfully say that creating SkillPath was the most fun I've ever had in my life, so I guess our goal setting worked!

- **Create happy campers:** Jerry and I decided that we were going to delight our employees by taking excellent care of them and fostering a fun, happy atmosphere at work. One way we took care of them was to offer health insurance from day one of employment, even when we had only a couple of employees. Later, through a ground-breaking agreement with Kaiser Permanente, we also obtained health insurance for same-sex domestic partners, long before this was routinely done. Since we eventually had many people working for us who were hearing impaired, we hired an interpreter for all SkillPath events so everyone would feel honored and included. We also offered free sign language classes to all employees, in case they wanted to broaden their skill sets and communicate better with all of their co-workers.

- **No jerks:** We both absolutely refused to work with people who were mean, difficult, pompous, irresponsible, or negligent. And this applied not only to employees, but to independent contractors and vendors, as well. If we disliked a person (or an organization), we'd simply find somebody to work with whom we *did* like. I have always held the belief—which has invariably proven to be true—that you can always find a qualified, talented person to fill any position who is *also* pleasant and fun to work with. These qualities are *not* mutually exclusive. There were two especially great benefits to our "no jerks" goal: We had more fun at work, and our employees always felt protected and supported by this policy.

- **No nonsense:** We decided to dispense with a lot of corporate rules that really didn't make sense to us. For example, since we had no walk-in traffic, we got rid of dress codes altogether. (Plus, the plain truth is that Jerry and I really preferred wearing jeans!) Our seminar leaders and public support staff needed to look conventionally professional because they were visible to our audiences; for the rest of us, the rule was "just be comfortable." We also decided that working with friends and family was okay; in fact, we encouraged it! Some of our best employees were brought in by family members who were already working for us, and to this day, we have husbands and wives, mothers and daughters, and brothers and sisters successfully working side by side at SkillPath. (And we've had more than a few people meet their life partners at SkillPath!) We also got rid of recurring meetings. Our rule was: If you need to have a meeting with somebody, set one! Most of our meetings ended up occurring spontaneously in the hallway. As for lunch meetings with vendors and suppliers, we simply didn't do them (much to other people's surprise), because we found them to be a waste of time.

■ *Class act:* This last goal is probably the most conventional of all the ones that we came up with—the kind you might find in the ideologies of many other organizations. We agreed that everything we did, big or small, would be top-notch. We vowed that our trainers would be excellent; that our workbooks, handouts, books, audio and video recordings, brochures, and catalogs would be letter-perfect; that our employees would be smart, well-informed, and pleasant—especially on the phone; and that we would provide the best, most informative seminars possible for our attendees. We were willing to spend plenty of time and money to reach this goal, and we instilled our vision of excellence in every one of our employees.

You may notice that there's one goal that's conspicuously missing from our list: Making a ton of money. Yes, we wanted to be successful, but making loads of money was never our primary aim. So SkillPath's financial success, and thus ours, was actually a secondary benefit of doing the right things as leaders, and of setting the right goals and achieving them.

Once we set our goals, we also set our deadline: Jerry and I wanted SkillPath to be completely up and running by the time we gave our first seminar, which we scheduled to take place just five months later. Believe me, five months isn't much time for two people to come up with a corporate infrastructure, beautiful brochures, excellent trainers, great workbooks, a computer system to track the seminar data, and books and audio recordings (which we produced ourselves) to be sold in the back of the room. But somehow, we did it. And in September 1989, in Phoenix, Arizona, we launched our first seminar, "Management and Supervisory Skills for Women," with over 300 people in the audience.

Setting goals that were reasonable, specific, measurable, adjustable, and meaningful to us gave us structure. Adding a time frame fired up our motivation. All we had to add was know-how and plenty of hard work. In a nutshell, that's how we built the company that I'm so proud of today.

If You Haven't Yet Found Your Dream Job ...

Okay, let's say you've set your goals but you haven't yet found your dream job. In fact, you're far from it. You may be a gofer for some autocrat or sitting in a windowless room, inputting reams of data in a huge IT department or literally scrubbing floors. Well, here's a little secret: Whatever it is you're doing, no matter how insignificant it may seem, if you do it with excellence, you'll be noticed. And you may even be promoted.

If you want to stand out from the crowd and move ahead, no matter what your current position, do the following:

- ■ *Be the best at something.* Because it's so unusual to see a person who *really* excels at her job, someone in the higher echelons is inevitably going to think, "Hmmm, I wonder whether we should consider her for another position ..." That's why you should set your sights on being the very *best* sandwich maker, floor scrubber, or assistant-to-the-assistant you can possibly be. It may not be a glamorous job right now, but if you demonstrate excellence, it's highly likely that you'll move up—and probably sooner rather than later.

- ■ *Meet your responsibilities.* One of my mentors once told me, "Just show up on time and do your job, and you'll be ahead of 90 percent of the other people." And, in the working world, I'm afraid it's all too true. However, this makes it that much easier for *you* to look great. So be punctual, always. And take your job responsibilities seriously; see to it that your work is completed properly and on time. It's amazing what a good impression you'll make simply by doing what you're supposed to do.

■ ***Do more than you're asked—and do so cheerfully.*** When Rachael Ray was in her early twenties and selling fancy foods at a gourmet food shop in Albany, New York, she noticed that her well-to-do customers bought prepared foods but shunned the grocery aisles. That's because they either didn't know how to cook or didn't want to spend the time. So Rachael started doing in-store demonstrations, showing her customers how to make quick, delicious, no-fuss meals. Her demonstrations became wildly popular and sold out quickly, and it wasn't long before a local TV station asked Rachael to do a regular segment featuring her "30-minute meals." Her career as a TV food star was on its way.

Rachael's demonstrations were her own idea, the result of her boundless energy and enthusiasm. And you can do the same. Look around your workplace and see what needs to be done. Is there a problem you might be able to solve? A mess you can clean up? A way you can improve things, not only for yourself, but also for others? Do *more*— it's a great way to get noticed.

■ ***Say "yes" to things nobody else wants to do.*** I may have a PhD in psychology, but I began my career on the very bottom rung—as an aide in a psychiatric hospital. Almost immediately, I became a psychiatric assistant, but my job duties were far from glamorous: I got the patients up and dressed, fed them, took their vital signs, broke up altercations (they often hit each other, and us, the staff), supervised smoke breaks (which meant I had to light everyone's cigarettes and make sure they didn't smoke them down to their fingers—and I truly hate cigarette smoke), and many other similar chores. I also had to clean up lots of messes of all kinds. (Go ahead and let your mind wander—you know what I'm talking about!)

Early on, I vowed to stay pleasant, no matter what, and often volunteered to take on patients who were combative and difficult. It was rough, tough, physical work, but I loved the patients and they loved me back. One day, there was a particularly bad smell coming out of a locked closet assigned to a patient I'll call Alice. She was difficult, violent, and almost impossible to handle, but she liked me, so I volunteered to go into her closet and find out what was going on. There was just one big problem. Alice could become extremely agitated and aggressive if anyone touched her body or her possessions.

As gently as possible, I tried to explain to her that something in the closet had gone bad and we needed to find out what it was and get rid of it. Alice protested and cried, but finally relented; then a few of us donned gowns, masks, and gloves and approached her closet. I unlocked the door and made a gruesome discovery—stacks and stacks of used sanitary napkins. Alice didn't want to throw them away because they were "part of her body." I pulled the ghastly mess out by myself, piece by piece, and the other staff members carted it away. Yeah, it was pretty gross. But I did it anyway, with as much professionalism, positivity, and empathy for Alice as I could muster. And I believe my willingness to tackle all kinds of chores like that one helped to make me a standout— showing that I was a team player, a hard worker, and the kind of person who could handle just about anything. It was undoubtedly a major reason that I moved up fast in that organization, becoming corporate clinical director while still in my twenties.

Countless people have climbed the career ladder this way—by taking on clients no one else wanted to deal with, doing dirty jobs, staying late, and working on holidays when everyone else was off having a good time. It might be unpleasant or even difficult, but it can solidify your image as a go-to person—one who can accomplish the impossible and work with the unmanageable.

- **Take chances.** Once you've chosen a direction, you'll encounter many forks in the road—times when you can either play it safe or go out on a limb. In most cases, I think it's best to go out on a limb; that's where you're more apt to reap the benefits. For example, when an enticing job opportunity arises, go for it—especially when you're young. Hanging on to your current job because it's safe and provides a regular paycheck can lead to years (or an entire career) spent stuck in the same position. In large corporations, there's an adage that often holds true: To reach a higher position, you sometimes have to go away and then get hired back. This means that the longer you sit in your current job, the more likely you'll be viewed as a person who can handle only that position. In short, if opportunity beckons and it looks reasonable, take a chance! Almost everyone who has ever moved up the career ladder has taken a gamble like this while reaching for the stars.

Keep Moving

As Albert Einstein said, "It is the same with people as it is with riding a bike. Only when moving can one comfortably maintain one's balance." The same is true with your goals. Keep pursuing them, and then set new ones as soon as the old ones are either realized or discarded. Always do your best, take the jobs no one else wants, think of new ways to improve the current situation for yourself and others, and plow ahead. You'll get somewhere eventually, although it might not be the exact destination you'd originally imagined. Still, doors *will* open for you, as long as you continue to walk down that hallway.

CHAPTER 2

POSITIVITY AND PASSION— TWO KEYS TO SUCCESS

Here's something I discovered over the years: Success is almost always the result of two things—*positive thinking*, the belief that you can and will achieve your goals, and *passion*, the energy, enthusiasm, and drive you need to get to the finish line. If either is in short supply, reaching your goals will be a whole lot harder, if not impossible. Nothing can derail you faster than doubting yourself, waffling, or beating yourself up for things you've done wrong. And if your passion wanes (or, God forbid, runs dry), facing and overcoming the challenges you'll encounter can become overwhelming.

So here's my first and greatest piece of advice: Muster as much positive energy and passion about your goals (and *yourself*) as you possibly can, because you're going to need it! And I'll take it even one step further: Become positive and passionate about *everything you do in life*. The rewards you reap will be endless. I know this empirically, because positive thinking and passion have played crucial roles in every single one of my achievements, and I'm sure they will for you, as well.

What's So Great About Positive Thinking?

Studies have shown that people who think positively do better in almost every area of life—that includes school, work, sports, relationships, you name it. But why? Is simply looking on the bright side enough to catapult you into the winner's circle in every walk of life? Research done by psychologist Barbara Fredrickson indicates that, yes, positive thoughts *can* put you over the top in your quest for success for two reasons: They expand your possibilities and build important skills that can serve you for a lifetime.

Fredrickson calls this the broaden-and-build theory. It works like this: Positive emotions *broaden* your sense of what's possible and open your mind. This provides solid ground for the *building* of valuable new skills and the discovery of new resources. In other words, because you're open and receptive to new things, you can grow and make connections more easily. And here's the great part: The broaden-and-build effect results from *all* kinds of positive thinking, not just saying to yourself, "I think I can. I think I can … " like *The Little Engine That Could*. This means that *any* thoughts that stir up your feelings of joy, interest, contentment, or love can get you going in the right direction.

How does this work? According to Fredrickson's studies, joy makes you want to play; interest makes you want to explore; contentment makes you want to savor and integrate; and love makes you want to do all of these within the safety of your closest relationships. These activities broaden your attention, cognition, and action, while building your intellectual, physical, and social resources. So the more positive thoughts you have, the more likely you are to experiment, explore, come out of yourself, connect with others, and take your place in the world—greatly increasing your chances of success!

And what do negative thoughts do? Just the opposite. They make you more guarded, anxious, depressed, aggressive, and inclined to contract rather than expand. So you'll be less likely to experiment, explore, or connect with others, which will lessen your chances of building intellectual, physical, or social resources—and lessen your chances of success. It makes sense: If you're using your time and energy to defend yourself against your real or imagined enemies (the primary impetus for negative thinking), you're not going to grow much, broaden, or make many valuable connections.

Positively Optimistic

Fortunately, thinking positively hasn't been a problem for me. I've always been the kind of person who looks on the bright side of situations. I also love to laugh and often find the humor in things that leave some people staring at me and wondering what could be so funny. Thanks to my natural inclinations and a supportive family environment, I grew up feeling that I could succeed at anything if I worked hard enough and stayed positive. And I believe my life has been blessed in every arena because of this.

A good chunk of my happiness and positivity was undoubtedly genetically transmitted to me from my mother, who was adored by everybody, but a lot of it was definitely learned behavior. Studies on positivity confirm that it's partly hardwired into the brain, but also partly an acquired mindset. This means that even those who are very much inclined toward optimism—say 60 percent of their positivity is due to underpinning—still have another 40 percent that can be learned. And that's good news, especially if you have a "glass-half-empty" personality, and you're closer to 30 percent hardwired toward optimism. You can still become more optimistic simply by changing your negative thoughts to positive ones. Happily, there's a well-established procedure for doing just that.

Turning Negative Into Positive: It's Easier Than You Think!

You *can* change your negative thoughts into positive ones, but first you'll need to become aware that they exist. Your thoughts are like a never-ending late-night talk radio show, rambling on and on, zipping from topic to topic. They can be so easy to ignore that you're barely aware of them. Yet they strongly affect your moods, values, personality, self-esteem, and actions. That's why it's important to tune in to what's currently playing in your head as often as possible. Some of it, you'll find, is just automatic thinking—how to get to the grocery store, parallel park your car, pay a bill, or load the dishwasher. These thoughts probably don't affect the way you feel about yourself or the likelihood that you'll reach important lifetime goals. Rather, it's the messages you send yourself *about* yourself that are vitally important, and they are the ones that need to be monitored and examined carefully.

Tune in to your thoughts— especially the negative ones

To increase your awareness of what's going on in your mind, I strongly suggest you keep a thought-monitoring journal. Tune in to your negative thoughts especially, and write them down. (While you're at it, go ahead and write down the positive ones too, on another page or in a separate journal. They're equally important to examine—and to celebrate! For the purposes of this exercise, however, let's keep talking about the negative ones.) Notice important career-related thoughts that are negative, like, "You're never going to get that job" or "It's impossible to move up around here." And pay particular attention to negative thoughts that relate to you as a person, like, "I'm so lazy about exercising; no wonder I'm out of shape!" or "These glasses make me look awful; I'm so ugly!" or "I did a dumb thing today."

You might be surprised at how many negative messages you send yourself. And while you may think that self-criticism can help you improve, it actually does just the opposite and can do much to block your success. Once you become aware of some of your negative thoughts, look for patterns. Perhaps you're hardest on yourself in the evenings after a long day's work or maybe in the mornings, when you've just rolled out of bed. Maybe most of your negative self-talk is centered on your work-related talents, or perhaps you're most critical concerning your personal skills. By keeping a thought-monitoring journal, you'll heighten your awareness of what's going on inside your head and when you're most inclined toward negative thinking.

Reexamine and reframe your negative thoughts

The next step is to zero in on one of your negative thoughts and examine its validity. Ask yourself: Am I exaggerating? Am I sending myself hurtful, unnecessary messages? If the answer is "yes" to either of these, your job is to reframe the thought—that is, to change it from negative (hurtful) to positive (constructive).

For example, let's say your car has broken down. You say to yourself:

> *Me and my bad luck! This is going to cost a fortune! I'll be without wheels for a few days, and I'll have to beg for rides from people. There's always something bad happening to me!*

Whoa! Let's reexamine all of these thoughts and assess their validity. Okay, it may be true that you'll have a big bill to pay and you'll be without a car for a while. But is this really due to your own terrible luck? And is your luck really bad, or does everyone have car trouble now and again? Finally, will you really have to *beg* for rides? Certain people may be quite happy to help you out.

If you've discovered that some of your thoughts aren't necessarily true and *are* unnecessarily negative, reframe them to make them more accurate and positive. For example, you might reframe the car trouble thoughts this way:

> *Ugh, car trouble! It's expensive and inconvenient, but everyone faces it now and again. I guess this just happens to be my turn.*

Now, go one step further to see if you can put a more positive spin on the experience, as in:

> *This gives me a chance to get my car thoroughly checked out and back into shape.*

> *I'll rideshare with my friend Samayah, who I don't see often enough. It'll be fun.*

> *This could be the wake-up call I needed to spur me to buy a new car.*

Most situations have both positive and negative sides, and I don't know how to emphasize this enough: *What you see will depend mostly on what you're looking for.* So make a concerted effort to look for the positive and muscle through the negative. The way you think really *is* a choice! You *can* control your thoughts.

Here are a few examples of career-related thoughts that can slow you down, plus positive—yet realistic—substitutions that can help you forge ahead:

- *I'm not smart (or strong, attractive, well-connected, outgoing, educated, driven, prepared, or organized) enough to get this job.*

  Substitute: *I have many great qualities and am a great candidate for this job.*

- *My project (idea, campaign, bid for a job, etc.) fell flat. I guess I should just give up.*

  Substitute: *Thomas Edison failed 1,000 times before inventing the light bulb. Failure is just a phase. Success awaits me, as long as I persevere.*

■ *I can't do this.*

Substitute: *I am capable of more than I realize. If I believe I can, I'm halfway there.*

■ *I'm too intimidated to try this. Therefore, I'll pass.*

Substitute: *If I face my fears, they will lessen and maybe even disappear.*

■ *This is just too much trouble for me to deal with.*

Substitute: *I have to deal with the challenges if I want to enjoy the successes.*

■ *I'm stuck in this job, and I'll never get anywhere.*

Substitute: *I'll be a stellar employee for another six months. Then, if nothing happens, I'll find another job.*

■ *If I can't do it perfectly, I might as well not do it at all.*

Substitute: *I'm setting the bar too high. If I'm more realistic and set it a little more sensibly, I'll have a much better chance of reaching my goals.*

■ *This is impossible.*

Substitute: *Things always seem impossible until you've done them. I'll keep trying.*

Negative Thinking Traps

Negative thinking can take many forms, but here are a few common thought patterns that can really bring you down and block your progress.

- **_Poor me:_** It's easy to fall into this one, convincing yourself that life is unfair, somebody has it in for you, or you're a victim of circumstance. Even if all of these happen to be true (and I seriously doubt they could _all_ be true!), wallowing in such thoughts can paralyze you. Remind yourself that whatever has happened is not necessarily a reflection on you personally. Then do whatever is necessary and forge ahead with confidence.

- **_The anger spiral:_** When confronted with unpleasant situations, some people go straight to the knee-jerk reaction of getting angry. Their anger builds until they're out of control or, at least, not functioning rationally. If you have a short fuse, be aware that blowing your top even once can jeopardize your career or your relationships with friends and family. Do your very best to keep your cool in all situations by realizing that anger is a choice. For example, let's say someone takes your parking space at work. You can choose to become furious, leap out of your car, and unleash an angry tirade on the other driver. Or you can say to yourself, "Wow, what a jerk! Oh well, there's another space down the way." You're not going to teach anybody a lesson by blowing up. But your mind, your body, and maybe your career can pay a heavy price.

- **_Fear of failure:_** Whenever you're faced with a new challenge, it's normal to feel a little apprehensive. You may wonder if you're really up to it or if you're going to fall flat on your face and look like an idiot. You might be taking big risks, putting your job, savings, and security on the line. Yet almost all success stories involve taking chances—often big ones. Tell yourself, "This may be scary, but I think I'm going to win." Then make the leap. If you don't venture out, you'll never know how far you could have gone. (But have a backup plan if possible—take a leave of absence rather than out-and-out quitting your current job, set aside the money you're willing to risk and don't spend more, pay off outstanding bills in advance, and so on.)

Beyond Positive Thinking— Changing the Hardwiring of Your Brain

Changing your negative thoughts to positive ones is an important step. But in order to make major changes in your outlook and behavior, you'll also need to change the "hardwiring" in your brain. Here's something that may surprise you: The human brain tends to be naturally hardwired toward the negative. This means that it pays much more attention to negative information—bad feelings, threatening experiences, and negative feedback—than to positive information. And there's a good reason for this: Zeroing in on the negative makes a lot of sense survival-wise.

Think about it: Prehistoric hunter-gatherers really needed to pay attention when something bad happened, or they could easily end up as somebody's dinner. So their brains were designed to set off alarm bells when something seemed dangerous or out of place—and the brain's structure was literally altered by negative experiences like fighting off wild animals, accidentally eating something poisonous, warring with enemy tribes, or suffering through a famine. These stressed-out hunter-gatherers became *reactive*—that is, more likely to jump to protective, stress-induced behaviors like anger, anxiety, hypervigilance, and depression or withdrawal. And when the dangerous situations occurred repeatedly, the reactive behaviors could be triggered by the smallest provocation. Thus, we descendants have become hardwired to look for the negatives within our environment.

Although we really don't need to leap to these protective behaviors very often in modern society, our brains are still hardwired like the hunter-gatherers. For example, let's say you've been cut off in traffic multiple times. After enough of these experiences, you become primed to see other drivers as the enemy every time you get behind the wheel. Then, when another driver does something you think is wrong or unfair, you go ballistic.

Or let's say you've been in the middle of some do-it-yourself home repair disasters. And now, every time you pick up a screwdriver, you're pretty sure you won't be able to do the job correctly. Just one overly stubborn screw will be enough to make you start swearing and thinking about giving up.

In each of these cases, your brain, already hardwired toward the negative, has remodeled itself to become even more negative toward activities that seem threatening to you. So you automatically go into the reactive mode whenever you face them.

Positive rewiring

The good news is that the brain can also remodel itself in response to *positive* experiences— just not as quickly or easily. To illustrate, let's go back to our stressed-out hunter-gatherers, who have now found themselves a safe haven with fresh water, plenty of fish, loads of berries and roots, and no enemies or threatening animals in sight. Safe and protected, with their basic needs met, the hunter-gatherers no longer feel threatened and begin to relax. Flooded with positive feelings, their brains slowly remodel themselves to become less reactive. After a while, instead of automatically leaping to protective behaviors when confronted with stressors, the hunter-gatherers face these situations more calmly and rationally.

Similarly, let's say you, the person who approaches do-it-yourself projects with trepidation and negativity, suddenly have a new next-door neighbor who is a great fix-it person. She helps you learn a few practical techniques, lends you the perfect tool for a certain job, and shows you how to use it. You find that, with her assistance, you can put up a light fixture or fix that loosened table leg with ease. After you've had several positive do-it-yourself experiences, you begin to feel confident, even eager, to tackle other projects. That's because your brain has rewired itself from the negative to the positive in this specific area.

There's just one small catch: It takes many more positive experiences to counteract a negative experience and rewire the brain. (Some researchers say five, others say even more.) Evidently, your very clever and hardworking brain needs to get the message several times over that "all is well" before it gives up its protective stance. So the more positive experiences you have (and this definitely includes *thinking* positively), the greater your chances of rewiring your brain for the better.

"Taking in the good"

Rick Hanson, a neuropsychologist and author of the book *Hardwiring Happiness: The New Brain Science of Contentment, Calm, and Confidence*, came up with a way to change the brain to become more positive and increase happiness. It's based on the idea that thoughts start to become experiences if you focus on them for a long enough period, say for at least 10 to 20 seconds. And the more often you do this, the more likely it is that the experience will become part of the hardwiring in your brain. That's because the neural structure is built through repeated patterns of mental activity—it's how we learn.

Hanson refers to his method as "taking in the good," he and breaks it down into three steps.

1. **Focus on a good experience.** Naturally, the more positive experiences you have in life, the better. But just *thinking* about something that makes you feel good also counts. Focus on something wonderful that a loved one said to you recently or a pet who makes you smile. Perhaps you got an email or a text that made your day. Or you accomplished something challenging. All of these qualify as good experiences.

2. **Let the experience engulf you.** Submerge yourself in the experience, and allow yourself to feel its full effects for 10 to 20 seconds. Sit back and really enjoy it—go ahead and smile a while! (We'll talk more about smiling later and its positive effects on your mind and body.)

3. **Absorb the experience.** Let it seep into your brain and body, all the way to your inner core. Soon, the experience will morph into a feeling and will actually start to change your neural structure—that is, it will become hardwired into your brain.

If you do this regularly, you can actually *teach* your brain to think more positively. And seriously, how cool is *that?*

Passion—Putting Your Positivity Into Motion

It's one thing to think positively, but quite another to convert your thoughts into something tangible—like a career, a business, a family, a garden, or any other goal you decide to pursue. That takes energy, and plenty of it! And the greatest source of energy in the world is passion, a strong feeling of enthusiasm or excitement for something. Passion can take you beyond whatever you've dreamed you could accomplish. It can give you the energy to do whatever you want to do—and more. And it can keep you focused and moving steadily forward for decades, sometimes even for a lifetime.

If you feel passionate about something, you might spend hours working at it without even noticing. You might find yourself gravitating toward it automatically whenever you have a little downtime—or even when you *should* be doing something else! You feel happy while engaged in this activity and find opportunities to come back to it whenever you can. In short, you love what you're doing and have energy to burn for this particular activity or interest. (By the way, that's exactly the way I've felt while writing this book!)

If you're lucky, you may already know what you're passionate about. If so, you probably also realize that it's closely related to your abilities. For example, let's say you just love softball. Chances are, you're really good at running, hitting, catching, and throwing. Or let's say your passion is fashion design. That's probably because you have a great imagination, a wonderful sense of color, and a good deal of originality. Or maybe you love the rough-and-tumble challenge of legal negotiations. In that case, it's likely that you happen to be skilled at interacting with others and coming out ahead.

But some people simply don't know what they're passionate about. I've given countless talks on finding your true passion, and inevitably someone will say to me, "I'm not really passionate about anything. How can I discover what my true passion is?" And I always reply, "Focus on your strengths." You excel at certain things; you're naturally proficient in certain areas; you have innate talents. Your passion usually lies in these areas. (Not always, but usually, and it's a great place to start exploring.)

If you're wondering where to find your source of passion, ask yourself the following questions:

- What comes easily to me?

- What makes me feel a sense of accomplishment?

- What do other people recognize in me or compliment me about?

- What excites me?

- What gives me back more energy than I put out?

Most likely, your answers will point to your passions, or at least to areas you can develop into passions. But don't worry if your "true passion" still eludes you. Many highly successful people didn't find their calling until quite late in life. For example, Julia Child was 38 before she began to study cooking seriously. Colonel Sanders didn't start the Kentucky Fried Chicken® chain until he was 65. The renowned American folk artist Grandma Moses was 78 before she started to paint in earnest. And Laura Ingalls Wilder (author of the *Little House* books) didn't publish her first book until she was 65.

It's never too late to find your passion! Just think about what you love to do; then do it and see how you feel. The energy and personal satisfaction you experience will guide you in the right direction as you explore the possibilities.

Pairing Passion With Career

If you can turn your passion into a career, you'll soar—no doubt about it. You'll happily work your tail off, while doing something you think is really fun. You'll do a great job, and you will rise, no matter what your profession. That's because your passion will give you the energy and drive to do whatever you need to do to get ahead and more. Just look at ballet dancers or actors who gladly spend 8 to 10 hours a day, 6 to 7 days a week, taking classes, rehearsing, or performing. Or marathon runners who push past their pain and exhaustion to run 26 long miles— and not just during a race, but several times a week throughout their training periods. Or writers who continue to polish the umpteenth version of their novels, with no guarantee they will ever be published or bring in a single penny. In all of these cases, it's passion that gives these people the energy and willpower they need to persevere.

No wonder we've all heard maxims like these: "Do what you love, and love what you do," "Passion is the difference between a job and a career," and "Follow your passion, and success will follow you." Passion is an important key to success.

When passion and work don't go hand in hand

Unfortunately, not all passions lend themselves to practical careers. It's quite possible that doing what you love isn't going to bring in enough money to support your lifestyle (remember that softball example?) or that you've been unable to pair your passion with your career for other reasons. Instead, you've found yourself working in an area that does not inspire passion within you; in fact, it may be just the opposite. Well, you're not alone. I recently read a survey of people who were engaged in quite desirable lines of work (dentists, electricians, etc.), who were asked, "Do you find joy and meaning in your career?" (To me, joy and meaning are nearly synonymous with passion.) Can you guess how many people said "yes"? Just 20 percent—one out of five!

You may be thinking, "Well, that's a total bummer. If passion is so important to career success, but only one in five people is passionate about what she does, what chance do I have?" I'm here to tell you: *You have every chance.* Why? Because passion, like positive thinking, is a learned behavior. And you can develop passion for whatever it is that you do. Your day-to-day job may be less than thrilling, but if you make a conscious effort to become passionate about it and perform to the best of your ability, it will have amazing effects on the way you feel and are seen by others. Your energy levels will increase, you'll accomplish more, you'll enjoy your job more, and you may even be considered for a promotion. Becoming passionate about what you do is the first step toward moving ahead!

I once knew a security guard named Martin whose main job was to direct traffic in the parking garage of a large corporation where I was doing some consulting work. Martin threw himself wholeheartedly into this seemingly boring position, enthusiastically waving "good morning" and "good night" to every person who drove by, directing traffic with energy and attention to detail, high-fiving other employees as they walked to their offices, and generally reveling in being the star of his own show. He was a blast to watch in action, and I always looked forward to his enthusiastic "hellos" whenever I'd arrive at work. Soon everyone knew Martin's name and spoke fondly of him. And it wasn't long before Martin was promoted to manager of the security department. Do you suppose Martin was truly passionate about directing traffic when he was given that assignment? My guess is he was not. But he became passionate, and in so doing, he thrived.

Increasing the passion factor

How can you become more passionate about what you do, even if it's not your favorite thing? Try the following:

- **Throw yourself enthusiastically into your duties.** It's so true that the more you put into something, the more you'll get out of it. Don't hold back. Channel Martin!

- **Act as if you're already passionate about what you're doing.** This is one of those "fake it 'til you make it" things, and it totally works. It really *will* help you muster true passion, because of an interesting and useful behavioral fact: Behavior *always* precedes emotions and feelings. In other words, *act* as if you are passionate, and you will eventually *feel* passionate.

■ ***Find creative ways to accomplish routine tasks.*** Put your own unique spin on your job, as long as it's within the realm of what's considered acceptable at your workplace. You'll be more energized, and maybe even entertained.

■ ***Look for learning opportunities so you can keep growing.*** The more you learn and grow, the more interesting your job (and you) will become. Beware of stagnation; it's a passion killer.

■ ***Create a positive aura around yourself.*** Make sure you think positively, put out only positive energy, and surround yourself with positive people. Negative thoughts, energy, and people will drain you and hold you back. (And while you're thinking about this, give your personal life a good look-over, as well. Negativity is crippling and debilitating wherever you encounter it, including in your relationships with acquaintances, friends, and family members.)

■ ***Practice selflessness, and give more than you get.*** Surprisingly, both will invigorate you and ignite your passion. You will find almost boundless satisfaction and energy by making the world a better place through your caring and compassion.

■ ***Laugh about your troubles, whatever they may be.*** Obviously, this isn't always possible, especially if you're feeling tired or frustrated. However, it may be more feasible than you might think. You may need some time and distance from problem situations before you can do this, but if you can have a good laugh at what's bothering you, it will seem less daunting. I do this as much as possible, and it works!

All of the above will help you find and increase your passion—something you'll need in large quantities in order to achieve your goals. Just choose one or two suggestions, and see what happens!

Combining Positivity and Passion to Reach Your Goals

I have always been a passionate person. In fact, if I feel ambivalent about something, it's usually a sign I'm on the wrong track. I love to throw myself into whatever I'm doing and make it the most important thing in the world at that moment—and I truly can't think of another way to approach life.

As with positive thinking, my passionate nature seems to be something I was born with. However, I'm equally sure that much of my passion is a *learned* behavior—most likely modeled for me by my very passionate father, who loved life more than anyone I've ever met. Still, there have been times when my naturally sunny disposition was challenged, and I've had to work hard to hold on to both my positivity and my passion.

The most clear-cut example is when Jerry and I decided to start SkillPath. Everyone we knew thought it was a bad idea—and not just our competitors, but also our friends, family members, and anyone who knew anything at all about the seminar business. "The market is already saturated with seminar companies," they told us. "Seminar companies are going under; there's not enough business to support them." "There's nothing new under the sun. How are you going to stand out?" "What makes you think you can compete with the big boys, especially the ones who have a 10-year jump on you?"

Literally, not a single person encouraged us.

Jerry and I simply had to press on without support, believe in ourselves, and reaffirm our goal of being the best seminar company in the business. If we'd listened to the naysayers, we would have given up before we started or folded up our tent at the first sign of trouble. But we had faith in our vision, and ourselves, and we forged ahead.

In general, seminar companies cover topics that fall into the same basic categories: Time management, stress management, people management, and self-management. Jerry and I didn't expect to come up with brand-new categories; we would just do a better job on the standard ones. And we knew we could. We made sure that our seminars were packed with useful information; our trainers were the best in the business; our support staff was at the top of their game; and our brochures, catalogs, products, and workbooks were colorful, attractive, and professionally produced. One of our biggest advantages, oddly enough, was that we were the "new kids on the block," which attracted a certain amount of interest. But then, of course, we had to deliver.

It was fairly easy to take business from the mediocre companies. But we also had to go head to head with the biggies, like Dun & Bradstreet®, CareerTrack®, Padgett-Thompson, Fred Pryor Seminars, and our former company, National Seminars Training. Our goal was to come up with seminars that offered the latest and greatest information—timely topics that people were interested in *right now.* Jerry and I lunched together every day and brainstormed about how we were going to make our company stand out. Then, two or three times a month, we went to the major bookstores and checked out books on various topics. Those with the largest presence became the subjects of our new seminars. (And to this day, in case you're wondering what the world is currently interested in, head to a major bookstore and check out the bookshelves, or jump on Amazon® and type in "best sellers." You'll see almost instantly what's trending.)

For example, one day we noticed that the latest thing in the business section of Barnes & Noble® was a concept from Japan called Total Quality Management (TQM). Because seminar topics often have a very short life cycle, we quickly studied up on the topic. Then, as fast as we could, we developed marketing and training materials on TQM, hired and trained several presenters, and put our brand-new seminar on the road. It was a hit! (But only for a very short time, so it's good we got it to market so quickly.) We used the same process for many subsequent topics, including project management, training the trainer, and PC troubleshooting, to name a few. We were working around the clock, but Jerry and I were both positive and passionate and knew where we were headed. More importantly, we felt *certain* we would succeed.

Our next idea was to produce what we called "designer seminars." We worked with popular authors like John Gray (*Men Are from Mars, Women Are from Venus*), Jack Canfield and Mark Victor Hansen (*Chicken Soup for the Soul*), Stephen R. Covey (*The 7 Habits of Highly Effective People*), and the famous Washington, DC/White House business etiquette guru Letitia Baldrige (*New Complete Guide to Executive Manners*). We based our seminars on their best-selling books and ideas, paid them for the rights, and sometimes gave them a percentage of the profits from the seminars. Although we made very little money on these seminars due to the hefty payouts to the authors, we attracted new customers, gained positive attention, and built up our mailing lists, which are gold in the seminar business. And because we had exclusive rights to the use of these book titles in our marketing materials, our "designer seminars" had no competition whatsoever from the competing seminar companies.

Eventually, after all but two of its big competitors had gone out of business, SkillPath became the largest seminar company in the world. Our positive thinking, endless passion, and die-hard work ethic catapulted us to our goals and beyond. And when we became number one in the training industry, although we were extremely pleased, neither of us was all that surprised.

Positivity and passion were two of our greatest assets, giving us the power to achieve our goals and blow past them. And I promise they can do the same for you!

CHAPTER 3

"SELL YOUR BRAND" AND MAKE PEOPLE TAKE NOTICE

No matter what it is that's propelled you into the job market—you're just starting out, you're looking for something that's more interesting and challenging, or you're completely changing careers—one thing is certain: To get the position you really want, you'll have to do a top-notch job of selling yourself. And that will be an entire undertaking in itself—one that's tough, often exhausting, and nonpaying to boot. But if you complete this task successfully, you'll stand to gain benefits that play out over your entire career.

You begin by thinking long and hard about what it is that you truly want. And that's incredibly important. This is your *life* we're talking about—what you'll do for the majority of your waking hours, how much money you'll make, who you'll be spending time with, and what the future holds for you! So just grabbing any old job isn't going to cut it. You need to find a position that suits you, utilizes your skills and talents, reflects your worth, and offers you opportunities for growth. In short, you need to find the right fit for *you*.

Clarify What You Want

Back when I was a teenager, I spent a whole summer selling snow cones in a baseball park. Yeah, I know—not too exciting. But it was a job, and I needed to make some money. At the time, it didn't really matter what I did, as long as it was ethical, safe, and at least a little bit fun. So selling snow cones met my needs. (And to this day, I can make really nice, round snow cones—what a skill!) But beginning, changing, or enhancing a *career* is a very different matter. You want something in your desired field that will be fulfilling, rewarding, and possibly a stepping-stone to better things. But what kind of job will fit the bill?

When I interview job seekers, I like to ask them questions like, "What makes you happy? What's your dream job? Would you rather work inside or outside? Do you like being with people?" These are exactly the kinds of questions you should be asking yourself. The more you understand yourself and the kind of career that will suit you best, the greater your chances are of landing that career and becoming successful. So sharpen your focus. Take some time to dream up the kind of job that would really make you sing. Ask yourself:

- What exactly am I looking for in a job?

- Do I need to be surrounded by people, or would I rather work alone?

- Do I work well in groups?

- Do I like to work independently?

- Do I want to hold a managerial or leadership position?

- What kind of schedule am I willing to keep? Am I willing to work long hours? Weekends? Early mornings? Graveyard shifts?

- Are title and status important to me?

- Am I willing to travel for business? If so, how often?

- Would I move to a different part of the country, if necessary?

- Would I move out of the country, if necessary?

- How much money do I need (or want) to make?

- What kinds of employment benefits have to be included?

- How far am I willing to commute to and from the job?

- Does a job need to provide me with opportunities for advancement, or am I willing to stay put if other requirements are met?

Once you've answered these questions, sit down and write a complete description of the kind of job you want. List everything that it must provide, and then go over the list carefully. Is there anything you *don't* absolutely have to have? If so, cross it out. Your aim should be to keep your list of career requirements as simple and short (but accurate) as possible. The longer the list, the harder it will be to find a job that fits.

When you've zeroed in on what you really *must* have in a job, make another list of the jobs that interest you and seem to meet your criteria. Then, next to each one, write down exactly what you're looking for—whatever it would take to make this a "dream job" for you. Narrow it down to one sentence. For example, you might say, "I want an entry-level position in solar energy sales that pays at least $50K a year, doesn't require work on weekends, gives me a company car and medical insurance, and has opportunities for advancement."

When reviewing your descriptions of dream jobs, make a note of those that require credentials, degrees, and certain kinds of experience. Do you already have what it takes to be considered for these jobs? If not, and you're really interested in pursuing one or more of them, you'll need to get qualified first. But if you simply need to find a job right now, you must narrow your search to those you're already qualified for.

So let's say you're a viable candidate for a certain job that meets most (if not all) of your requirements. Great! Your next step is to set a time frame for finding such a position. Chasing a specific job or career for too long without changing your circumstances can be counterproductive, so put a limit on it. You might say, "I'll search for a job like this for six months. If I don't find one during that time, I'll revise my requirements." This doesn't mean you have to give up on the job permanently; just be flexible. You might need to get other kinds of experience or qualifications before would-be employers will sit up and take notice. Or you might need to set your sights on something that isn't quite so elusive.

Zero In on Your Target Audience

Once you've clarified what you want, start searching for employers who offer the kind of job you're seeking. But that's not all you should look for—the company culture must also suit your personality, skills, talents, and level of ambition. "Company culture" is more or less a mash-up of an organization's goals, ethics, and social/psychological environment, plus the kinds of employees it values.

Take Google®, for example. It's well known as a freewheeling company that eschews traditional hierarchy, values diversity, and encourages employees to speak their minds. Essentially, in the company culture, everyone is equal—at least in theory. The Google Web site says they're looking for employees who are "smart and determined," and they value "ability over experience." In other words, you might be hired even if you don't have a lengthy résumé, as long as you're very smart and capable. Google also touts its employees as people who "pursue interests ranging from cycling to beekeeping, from frisbee [sic] to foxtrot." Google® is basically saying that the culture is fun, creative, not stuffy, and probably young.

In contrast, investment banks on Wall Street undoubtedly have company cultures quite different from Google's. They are much more likely to value advanced degrees (like MBAs); résumés steeped in finance; and personalities that are serious, dedicated, and highly conventional. And, of course, in organizations like these, hierarchy is king; there's no pretense about everybody being equal.

It will be well worth your while to find out all you can about an organization's company culture before you decide to apply for a job there. Begin by searching the "Career/Jobs" and "Company Culture" sections of a company's Web site. Even if the company culture, per se, isn't discussed, most Web sites will offer something about the company's goals and ideals and the kinds of employees they're looking for. Of course, none of them are going to say anything about the company that's the least bit unflattering (e.g., "We're stiff, authoritarian, rule-bound, and uninterested in the human side of our employees."). So to find out more, you'll have to look elsewhere and dig deeper.

A good place to start is at job fairs, where real live employees are just dying to talk to you and answer your questions. These people will be more than happy to tell you about their companies and all they have to offer. Naturally, everything they say will be completely positive, but you can ask about the company culture and probably get a feel for what it's like by reading between the lines of what the recruiter tells you about her company. I'm a big fan of job fairs and think you should go to as many as you can, gather all kinds of information, and talk to anyone in a field even remotely related to the one that interests you. Not only is it educational, but it's great communication practice! Then, go home and research these companies on the Internet.

Generate Leads

By now you probably have a good idea of the companies you'd like to work for. But that doesn't necessarily mean those companies are looking to hire right now. What you really need is news of a job opening. This is referred to as a "lead," and you'll need to generate as many leads as you possibly can. Here are some of the best ways to do so:

- **Ask family, friends, or other contacts in your field of choice.** Your family members, friends, or other contacts may have inside information about job openings even before those jobs are posted. They may also be able to get you in to see the appropriate people and offer referrals and recommendations. As we all know, the best way to get a job is to know someone, so be sure to avail yourself of this kind of help!

- **Tell everyone you know that you're looking for a job.** Spread the news; you never know who can help you. It's always best to have face-to-face conversations, but phone calls, emails, handwritten notes, and social networking also work. (However, if you're currently working, you may not want to tell the people at your present company that you're looking for a new job, especially if you need to stay there while conducting your search. Sometimes companies can be touchy about this sort of thing.)

- **Troll Internet job sites such as monster.com.** I know, it's a long shot, but *somebody* gets hired this way.

- **Join LinkedIn® or other business social networking sites.** Post a description of your desired job, plus your résumé. You can also look for job openings on these sites.

- **Call companies and people you find interest in.** Here's another long shot, but if you really admire a certain kind of business, a company, or an individual, call them. Find out about hiring procedures and the possibility of getting an informational interview (an appointment with someone who will talk to you about the business, but isn't interviewing you for a job). You never know; they might like you and end up creating a space for you.

- **Join professional organizations.** The best way to learn about a certain profession is to hang out with those who are already inside. So if you want to be a writer, join the National Writers Association. If you want to get into marketing, join the American Marketing Association. There are also online interest groups and professional organizations you can join. Some of them encourage beginners to ask questions of the more experienced members—it's like having a cyber mentor!

- **Get an internship at a company that you love.** This is a great way to find out a lot about what it's like to work at a given company. And you'll certainly make plenty of contacts. Be sure to tell everyone you meet that you're looking for a job.

By this point, you've made some important strides: You've decided on the job you want, narrowed your list of potential employers to those that seem to be a good fit for you, and generated some decent leads. Next, you need to go into marketing mode.

Think of Yourself as a Product!

Even though you're a human being, once you enter the job market, you become a product: A package deal made up of your experience, talents, work habits, ethics, personality, communication skills, recommendations and, of course, ability to get the job done. Your job is to sell the entire package, not just your winning personality or your job history. You can start by pinpointing what makes you the perfect person for the job.

Figure out your USP (unique selling point)

Any advertiser worth her salt is going to figure out a product's unique selling point (USP) and broadcast it to the world. A car is touted as super-fast, sexy, trustworthy on slippery highways, or rough and tough enough to take on the back roads. Flavored water becomes the hippest, coolest, newest way to hydrate yourself. An all-in-one vacation package is your passport to the most impossibly idyllic beaches in the world. A USP is whatever makes a product stand out from its competitors—in a good way, of course. And that's what you need to sell yourself successfully: Your own USP. Fortunately, you've got at least one—if not several.

For example, let's say you're trying to land a position as a corporate trainer. During the past four years, you've belonged to Toastmasters, the public speaking club, and worked your way up to its highest level of competence. This is certainly a USP! A toastmaster is a trained, experienced speaker.

Or let's say you've got your eye on a management position in your current company, even though you've never been a manager before. What do you have to offer that shows you can be an excellent manager? Oh yes, you were a lieutenant in the Army for six years. That's definitely a USP that demonstrates your leadership skills.

Think back on all you've done in your life, and ask yourself what you might use as a USP. Perhaps you've worked with children, volunteered for Habitat for Humanity®, spent two years in the Peace Corps®, earned a degree in communication, or taught English to ESL students. Or maybe it's something you've pursued since childhood—a hobby or an interest—that shaped you in a certain way that makes you an excellent candidate for a job.

I know a brilliant young woman named Deborah, and her backstory perfectly illustrates this concept. Deborah was a ballet dancer. She started ballet lessons at age three, spent her childhood and teenage years training and performing, joined the Joffrey Ballet company at 18, and became a soloist two years later. Unfortunately, just six months after that, she suffered an ankle injury that ended her career.

Not one to be kept down for long, Deborah enrolled in college, got a degree in political science, and went to law school. Then, with her JD in hand, she applied for a position at the district attorney's office in Los Angeles. She didn't have any trial experience. Although she did well in law school, she wasn't at the top of her class and didn't make law review. However, her training and experiences as a ballet dancer made her exactly the kind of person well suited to a career in the courtroom.

Deborah's USP was her ballet background. And when she was called in for an interview, she was easily able to use her USP to draw parallels between a professional dancer and a trial attorney. Both, she explained, are:

- Highly disciplined, mentally and emotionally
- Controlled
- Persistent
- Reliable
- Able to work well under intense pressure

- Quick to pick up information and patterns
- Excellent at connecting emotionally with an audience
- Skilled at improvising, especially when things go wrong
- Adept at working with others
- Able to forgo instant gratification in favor of long-term rewards

Deborah had spent a lifetime developing the same skills that are highly prized in trial attorneys. In short, she was a natural. Once she explained this to her prospective employer, she got the job.

Know three reasons why they should hire you

A USP is essential, but you'll need more than that. At some point, every interviewer is going to ask, "Why should we hire you?" And you'll need to come up with some good reasons why *you* are exactly the person they're looking for. It's very tough to think up good reasons on the fly, especially if you, like most of us, aren't used to talking yourself up. So, well in advance of an interview, come up with a list of three specific characteristics or accomplishments that show you are an excellent fit for the position.

If your USP happens to be a former career or long-standing interest, like Deborah's ballet dancing, you might be able to look to it for your three reasons. You might ask friends and family what they think. Then put yourself in the interviewer's shoes and think about what he may be looking for. (Review that job description!) Tailor your list of reasons to match.

Once you've settled on your three reasons, come up with examples for each. People love to hear stories, as long as they don't go on too long. So if one of your reasons is "I can work successfully with the most difficult clients," go ahead and tell them about the tough client who loved working with you—and only you.

Memorize your three reasons and the stories behind them. Your reasons, plus your USP, are your ammunition, the cache you'll be able to draw from to answer at least some of the interviewer's questions. They are selling tools that clearly demonstrate to the employer why you're special and why she should hire you. So know your reasons and examples backward and forward. Then you'll be well prepared to sell a unique product—yourself!

The All-important Résumé

Your résumé—a written summary of your skills, abilities, and accomplishments—is a primary job-search marketing tool. And just like a good advertisement, it should catch the eye of the potential buyer and describe or demonstrate what the product (you) can do for her. In the best of all possible worlds, when a prospective employer finishes reading your résumé, she will immediately grab the phone and call you in for an interview.

It begins with a cover letter. Whether you're submitting your résumé via email or sending a hard copy, the cover letter should be personalized. (No form letters!) Include the full name and address of the person you're contacting; begin with "Dear Ms. (or Mr.) _____ "; and include a brief, polite statement of the reason that you're writing, stating your desire to set up an interview with him or her (e.g., "I'm interested in applying for the position of _____ and have attached my résumé. I would be happy to meet with you at your convenience to discuss this opportunity.") Use a formal closing, such as "Sincerely," "Best regards," or "Best wishes," followed by your full name. If you're sending a hard copy, include a handwritten signature, in blue ink, above your typewritten name. (Blue ink instantly demonstrates that it's a real signature and not a printed one.)

As for your résumé, there's really no "correct" form—it varies quite a bit depending on the field. If, for example, you're applying for a job marketing the hippest hair salon in SoHo, your résumé will probably look much different than if you're applying for a job in a senator's office. But generally, a résumé has four main parts:

1. A summary of your qualifications (your most important qualities and abilities)

2. A list of your skills and accomplishments (jobs held, achievements relevant to the job being sought, awards received)

3. Your education

4. Your references

I'm no expert in résumé writing, so I'm not going to provide you with formats to copy or examples of what I think are ideal résumés. There are entire books and lots of Web sites (many of them free) that can help you figure out how to come up with a great-looking résumé. You can even hire a professional to write it for you. I do, however, consider myself an expert on *reading* and *evaluating* résumés. I've hired hundreds of people and read every one of their résumés. And I'm here to tell you that some of them are great and others are just terrible. Some can put me to sleep faster than Ambien®, while others are so riddled with typos and mistakes that I simply give up on them. Yet there are some that are so interesting and easy to read that they grab my attention from the get-go. In short, I know quite a bit about what works and what doesn't from the perspective of the *hirer*—and that's what I'm about to share with you.

Résumé dos and don'ts

When Jerry and I were creating advertising brochures for SkillPath, we knew we had only a few seconds of a person's attention before he decided to keep reading it or throw it away. The same goes for your résumé, which is typically read in 10 seconds. (Yes, that's the truth!) So your number one goal should be to make it as simple and clear as possible. Make it easy for a potential employer to see who you are and what you're selling in a glance. Reading résumés is a tedious job! Don't make it any harder than necessary, or yours may end up in the trash can.

With that in mind, here are my dos and don'ts when creating a résumé:

Dos

- Do use a simple Microsoft® Word format that's easy to read on most computers, instead of a template or table format that's hard to open. Believe me; if your résumé won't open instantly on a prospective employer's computer, it's unlikely that he'll bother with you.

- Do use a traditional font in black; I like Times New Roman, in 9- to 12-point size.

- Do be consistent in formatting or style.

- Do use high-quality, plain white paper for printed copies.

- Do put your name, address, phone number, and email address at the top of the page where they can be found easily. Don't make employers hunt for it!

- Do keep your résumé to one page, if at all possible. If you really must have two pages, staple them together, *and* put your full name and contact info at the top of the second page, in case the pages become separated.

- Do list your most recent (or present) job first in your work history, and then continue in reverse chronological order.

- Do list each company's complete name and location, what kind of business it is, and your dates of employment (e.g.,

June 2012 – September 2017). Then list your position and your accomplishments.

- Do use sentence fragments to describe your accomplishments (to save space). Begin with a verb (e.g., "Managed purchasing, invoicing, and tracking of supplies for department of 100+ employees." "Named salesperson of the year in 2015." "Increased sales revenue by 25%."). Accomplishments can also include the karate championship you won in 2009 or the first-place trophy you carried off at the state fair tap-dancing contest. Information like this is eye-catching and can make the interviewer want to know more. (Just avoid mentioning accomplishments of questionable notoriety, like the beer-chugging contest you won at last year's company picnic—unless, of course, you're applying for a job at a brewery!)

- Do have names and contact information ready to submit if you put "references available upon request" on your résumé. If you have room on the page, list the names and contact numbers of one professional and one personal reference. (Not your mom; they'll figure it out!)

Don'ts

- Don't use complex templates or formats.

- Don't use colored paper. Some résumé writing guides say that colored paper makes your résumé stand out from the crowd, and technically it does, but don't buy into that idea. It simply makes your résumé look gimmicky and unprofessional.

- Don't use fancy fonts; they're irritating and virtually unreadable.

- Don't overdo the use of italics, underlining, and bolding (also irritating).

- Don't bother listing "objectives." The interviewer already knows why you're there.

- Don't put a photo on your résumé (unless you're applying to be a model)—it can work against you.

- Don't put anything on your résumé that isn't true.

- Don't allow any typos, poor grammar, or punctuation mistakes to sneak through.

- Don't list anyone as a reference without asking first and being absolutely sure he or she will give you a glowing review.

- Don't assume references won't be called. I *always* call a prospective employee's references, and you'd be surprised at the lukewarm or even negative reports I've sometimes received!

Before You Send Out That Résumé ...

You need to be completely ready to start interviewing as soon as you send out your first résumé. Don't assume you'll have days or weeks to get your act together while you wait for the phone to ring—it might start ringing right away. (We can only hope!) So finish these tasks before you begin your marketing campaign:

- ***Gather impressive letters of recommendation.*** Ask former employers, business acquaintances, professors, teachers, or others *whom you know will extol your virtues* to write letters of recommendation for you. Then, don't use a letter unless it makes you seem impressive. Employers understand the concept of "damning with faint praise" (offering such marginal praise that it really isn't praise at all). Be sure you have your (excellent) letters of recommendation firmly in hand before you send out any résumés.

  And, as a quick aside, it's not unusual for a former employer or teacher to ask *you* to write your letter of recommendation, and then submit it to them for their approval. If this happens, don't be shy or self-effacing—talk yourself up! I promise it's not cheating to write your own letter, as long as it's authorized by the person who signs it.

- **Clean up your social networking sites.** Since it's almost a sure bet these days that a prospective employer will investigate your social media profiles, you must think of your Facebook® profile, Twitter® feed, LinkedIn® page, and the rest as extensions of your job application and résumé. Get rid of anything you wouldn't want a prospective employer (or your grandma) to see—incriminating pictures, sex talk, references to drinking and hard partying, or whatever. You can find plenty of information about this, with specific recommendations, by searching "cleaning up social networking sites" on the Internet. Don't skip this important step! Plenty of employers won't even set up an interview with you if they're turned off by what they find out online.

- **Make sure your email address and voice mail announcement sound professional.** Email addresses like *partyanimal@hotchix.com* or *darkwarlord@dnd.net* make you look immature and unprofessional (although I gotta give you credit for creativity!). Ditto silly voice mail messages or voice mail that answers for you and your sideline catering and pet-grooming businesses. Change your email address and your phone message to something standard that includes your full name and is appropriate to a solid, professional businessperson. And make sure you record a personal voice mail message. Nothing says, "I don't really care" more than that factory-recorded robot voice that begins with, "We're not available to take your call right now … "

■ *Shop for business attire that's attractive and low-key and fits you properly.* The way you look really counts! So start shopping for your interview outfit *now*. If you wait until your interview is scheduled to look for the "right" clothes, I guarantee you'll be rushing around in a panic and won't find exactly what you want. When selecting an outfit, ask yourself three questions: Is it appropriate for this particular job and organization? Am I sending the message that I'm competent and professional? Does it work for me?

The rule of thumb for an interview is to dress just a bit more formally and conventionally than you would for the job itself. But just how formally and conventionally depends on the position and the company. For example, the "right" look for a tech position at Apple® is going to be different (maybe a *lot* different) from the "right" look for a trial attorney at Jones Day®. To be on the safe side, call the company's HR department and ask about appropriate interview wear.

Make sure you "test-drive" your outfit at least once before the big day. During the interview, you'll have enough on your mind without tags poking you in the side or a collar choking you to death. If it doesn't look or feel right during your test-drive, you'll still have time to make a change.

How to Shop and Dress for an Interview

Here are six quick tips that apply to dressing for just about any interview:

1. Stay away from fads

2. Buy quality, durable clothing that resists wrinkling

3. Remember that neatness counts

4. Avoid distracting accessories

5. Make sure your outfit covers any tattoos

6. Wear what is comfortable for you!

In sum, the idea is to look as polished as possible without going over the top.

- **_Keep your hair trimmed and simply styled._** If you've got pink or blue hair, now is the time to opt for a more natural color, unless imaginative hair colors are well accepted in your chosen field. Stay current with your hair care so you don't have to rush out for a cut or color the day before your interview. And resist the urge to experiment with new hairstyles or color jobs—now is not the time for a hair disaster! Stick with what works.

- **_Remove your piercings, and find a way to hide your tattoos._** As with alternative hair colors, unless piercings and tattoos are considered absolutely 100 percent acceptable in your industry, it's a good idea to downplay them. So pull the gauges and lose the ink—at least for the interview.

Do I Care if You Have Purple Hair?

In two simple words, *absolutely not!* I actually love creative personal styles. If I were interviewing you, I honestly wouldn't care if you had purple hair, radical undercuts, piercings, tattoos, black polish on your fingernails, or any other "alternative" look. (There is one exception: SkillPath trainers have to present a professional, culturally neutral look to audiences so they don't distract from the message.) In general, I would focus much more on how well I thought you would perform for the company than how you styled yourself.

Unfortunately, that's not the way it typically works in the business world, where the "wrong" look (whatever that may be) can be enough to disqualify you immediately.

So throughout this book, regardless of my easygoing personal stance, I will always suggest that you present yourself in the most conventional way possible. It's certainly the safest option, and the one most likely to help you get your foot in the door. Look at it this way: It's *highly unlikely* that they won't hire you because you *don't* have purple hair, but it's *possible* that they won't hire you because you *do*.

■ ***Practice shaking hands.*** In the business world, shaking hands is a universal tool used to greet someone, demonstrate goodwill, and/or seal a deal. It also conveys something extra about your personality and confidence level, for better or worse. To make sure you're not sending the wrong message, ask a friend to help you practice the "right way" to shake hands.

Shake Hands Like a Pro!

Unless the Vulcan salute completely takes over within your lifetime (hey, it could happen!), you will be shaking hands with people almost daily. It's the most common way we greet others in professional settings, and it's also the most common way we greet another person, no matter what the occasion, when we first meet them (including first dates!). There are definite rules for shaking hands properly. Do it right, and you'll make a good impression from the start.

- **Extend your right hand toward the other person's right hand.** Don't be tentative, but don't rush in, either.

- **Point your thumb upward and toward the other person's arm.** Your arm should extend downward from elbow to wrist, at a slight angle.

- **Slide your hand all the way into the other person's palm, and wrap it around his or her hand.** Make sure the thumb joints and the palms of both parties' hands connect securely. (Offering just a part of your hand or, worse, only your fingertips, is a big turnoff because it seems timid and weak.)

- **Grasp the other person's hand firmly, and gently squeeze once.** Don't let your grasp be too limp, but don't make it a "bone-crusher" either.

- **Pump the other person's hand a time or two to show sincerity.** Pumping one to three times is the norm. Make sure the action originates in the forearm, not in the hand itself. The movement will be smoother and less jarring.

- **Hold the handshake for two to three seconds, and then break the grip.** Breaking sooner can give the other person the impression that you can't wait to get away. But holding on too long might seem overly intimate, which can be awkward and uncomfortable.

There are also specific behaviors that must accompany shaking hands:

- ■ ***Look the other person straight in the eye, and don't break eye contact.*** Looking away can make you seem insincere or lacking in confidence.

- ■ ***Smile.*** This conveys your friendliness and enthusiasm about meeting the other person.

- ■ ***Introduce yourself* before *extending your hand.*** This applies only if you're *initiating* the handshake, and it's the first time you've met. For example, I would say, "Hi, I'm Denise Dudley," *then* offer my hand. Leaping into a handshake while simultaneously introducing yourself can make you look rushed or overly eager. (Ignore this tip if you're *not* initiating the handshake, because you'll already be shaking hands before you have a chance to speak.)

- ■ ***Continue with pleasantries once you've begun the handshake.*** This is the point when you say things like, "It's great to meet you."

After you have all of this down, be sure to practice! Practice on your friends, your roommates, your mom, and even strangers—there's nothing wrong with offering a handshake to the person who helps you at the Apple Store® or the DMV; in fact, it's a kind and polite gesture. (Although I'll warn you that the DMV people are usually very surprised! They must not routinely get much love and attention—which is all the more reason to do it.) The more you practice, the more confident you'll feel about this very important business ritual. And trust me on this one—your interviewer will be evaluating your handshake, so you'll want to be well prepared ahead of time.

Ready, set, go!

At this point, you're polished and professional-looking, you know what you want, you're confident about what you have to offer, and you've presented your résumé to employers who appear to be a good match for you (and vice versa). Good job!

Now all you have to do is wait for that email or text to arrive or that phone to ring ...

CHAPTER 4

TURN YOUR INTERVIEW INTO A JOB OFFER

Finally, they've contacted you! A company that seems like an ideal match for you wants to interview you for a position you're really excited about. And you're ready to go: You know your unique selling point. You've got three reasons why the company should hire you (plus examples) firmly in mind. You've got letters of recommendation and a great outfit to wear that's professional and comfortable, and you can shake hands like a pro. But there are some important things you must do if you're going to make the best possible impression during your interview.

It starts as soon as you get the good news. The person who calls will probably want to set a time for the interview right away. And there are good times and not-so-good times for interviews. The best times are Tuesday, Wednesday, or Thursday mornings, first appointment of the day. Energy levels, concentration, and mood all tend to be better in the morning, and if you get the first appointment, the interviewer won't have to haul herself away from some other task to see you, which could put her in a negative frame of mind. If possible, stay away from Monday mornings, when most people are still dragging from the weekend, and Friday mornings, when some are mentally on "weekend time" already.

If you do get stuck with an afternoon appointment, try to get the earliest one available. The worst possible time is Friday afternoon; the interviewer may be exhausted from the week, psychologically checked out of work, and eager to escape. Do whatever you can to avoid this time slot!

Days (or Weeks) Before the Interview

The interviewer may want to see you tomorrow, or you might have weeks before your appointment takes place. Use whatever time you have to prepare yourself so you'll be as sharp and together as possible by doing the following:

- **Intensify your research on the company.** First, go over the information you've already gathered about the company, and then look for more. Find out about recent company and/or industry developments by doing an Internet search of the company's recent press releases. Call the company and ask for brochures or other information. If you know anyone familiar with the company, find out what he or she knows.

- **Review the job description.** Take another look at the job description and read between the lines. What do they *really* want? What can you do or say to show them you are a match for the job?

- **Go over your list of three reasons why the company should hire you.** Commit these to memory, and be ready with a good example of each.

- **Make a list of questions to ask about the company and the job.** You'll definitely be asked if you have any questions, so come prepared. This is a good opportunity to find out more about the company culture, the company's recent developments, the traits that distinguish it from its competitors, and how certain industry-wide changes are affecting it. If you like, you can also ask about salary, hours, and benefits, if these topics haven't already been discussed. But one question *not* to ask is, "How many days off will I get, including vacation and sick days, and how soon can I start taking them?" Queries like this can make it seem like you're already planning your escape!

The Day Before the Interview

You'll have a whole lot on your mind the day of the interview. To ensure that you're not scrambling around at the last minute, take care of these details in advance:

- **Check the time of your commute.** The day before, look at the traffic report on Google Maps® or other traffic sites at the time that you'll be traveling tomorrow. How long does the commute take at that time of day? Tack on an additional 45 minutes to an hour to this figure to make sure you won't be late.

- **Pack your binder or briefcase.** Make copies of your résumé, letters of recommendation, questions about the company, and other pertinent information. If you've been asked to bring samples of your work, a portfolio, or some other way to demonstrate what you've accomplished, be sure to include them. Whatever you bring should be neatly enclosed in a file folder, a binder, or a briefcase.

- **Lay out your clothes for tomorrow.** Make sure your outfit is pressed and ready to go, your shoes are shined (if necessary), and your accessories are in good shape. Ladies, if you're changing purses, transfer everything now. And if you're wearing pantyhose or tights, bring an extra pair in case the first pair runs.

- **Take care of your hands.** Be sure your nails are clean and neatly trimmed. Polish, if used, should be neutral—no wild colors or black, unless it's absolutely *de rigueur* within the industry you're entering.

- **Make sure your car is in shape.** If you're driving to the interview, see that there is plenty of gas in the tank and air in the tires. The last thing you need on the way to the interview is car trouble or an empty gas tank! Also, give your car a good cleaning, both inside and out. There is always the remote possibility that the interviewer may walk you to your car or the CEO will leave the building at the same time you do. (Trust me, it happens.)

- **Set your alarm to ring an hour earlier than you think is necessary.** You'll avoid oversleeping and can get ready at a leisurely pace.

Now, on to you personally. It's important that you get plenty of rest the night before the interview so you'll be at your peak mentally, emotionally, and physically. You can increase your chances of getting a good night's sleep by doing the following:

- **Get some exercise.** Go to the gym, take a brisk walk, or ride your bike so you can burn off stress hormones, release muscle tension, and prepare your body to relax. But don't exercise in the evening—you can rev up your body to the point of disturbing your sleep.

- **Avoid caffeine late in the day.** Depending on how caffeine-sensitive you are, you may need to stop all beverages, foods, and medications containing caffeine (this includes chocolate and certain headache remedies) as early as noon to keep from interfering with your sleep tonight.

- *Eat a well-balanced but light dinner.* Tonight is not a good night to suffer from indigestion! Stay away from heavy, greasy, or gas-producing foods. Also, stop eating at least two hours before bedtime, so your digestive system isn't still running at full bore when you're trying to sleep.

- *Avoid alcohol and recreational drugs.* Obviously, getting drunk or high is a bad idea the night before an interview. But even small amounts of these drugs can interfere with good sleep and make you less sharp tomorrow. In a word: Abstain. At least for tonight.

- *Wind down.* About an hour before bedtime, calm and center yourself by sitting quietly and doing some deep breathing. If you like, do some yoga stretches or meditate. Picture yourself in a calming, relaxing place where all is well. Imagine yourself sleeping well tonight.

- *Go to bed early enough to allow at least eight hours of sleep.* If that means you're hitting the sack at nine o'clock, so be it. And as you drift off, visualize your perfect self, calm, poised, and confident, acing tomorrow's interview. Visualization really works! Your brain and body are always "listening" to what you say to yourself, so think positively about tomorrow's outcome.

If, after making your best attempts, you find that you can't fall asleep, don't sweat it. Get up and do something mindless and routine like folding laundry. (Stay away from the computer or other visual electronic devices, because light promotes wakefulness.) Then, when you start to feel sleepy, go back to bed again. Take solace in the fact that just relaxing in bed for eight hours is worth a lot, even if your sleep quality is poor.

The Day of the Interview

The alarm goes off and, finally, the big day has arrived! You're all prepared—all you have to do is get up, put yourself together, and get to the interview on time. In the process, be sure to:

- **Eat a high-protein, high-fiber breakfast.** Skipping breakfast or grabbing a donut and a cup of coffee are *not* options today. For breakfast, choose high-protein foods like eggs and cottage cheese, plus high-fiber cereals and breads, to ensure a steady supply of glucose to your brain. This will keep your energy up and your brain sharp. Skip the onions and garlic, though, or anything else that might give you dragon breath.

- **Pay attention to your hygiene, hair, and makeup.** Take a shower, use deodorant, and avoid cologne or perfumed aftershave—some people are turned off by it or may even be allergic to it. Keep your hair and makeup neat and understated. As discussed earlier, remove piercings and hide tattoos, unless you're completely sure they're accepted at your prospective place of employment.

- **Bring your binder/briefcase and driving directions.** Set these all-important items right next to the front door where you'll see them on your way out and won't forget them. (It always works for me.)

- **Leave on time.** If you've added 45 minutes to an hour to the "normal" commute time, you'll most likely arrive way too early. But that's okay—you'll have plenty of time to park, relax, and gather your wits before you head to your appointment. You might want to bring headphones and listen to relaxing music while you wait. Or practice another visualization exercise: Close your eyes and imagine yourself calm, relaxed, and in control, nailing the interview, dazzling the interviewer, and landing the job!

- **Don't go to the office until 10 – 15 minutes before the interview.** The interviewer won't think it's cool if you show up half an hour early and camp out in the waiting room. She may feel pressured by your presence. So wait in your car. Or, if you've come via public transportation, wait in a nearby coffee shop.

- **Review your documents.** While you're waiting, refresh your memory by taking another look at your résumé, your USP, your three reasons plus examples, and the job description. If you have your mobile device handy, do one more Internet search of the company to find out if there have been any new developments. (If you can mention some breaking news about the company during the interview, you'll look sharp.) Once you've gone over everything, just sit and let this information settle into your brain.

- **Bring to the interview only what's absolutely necessary.** When you head to the office, take only your briefcase/binder and, for women, your purse. Leave your overcoat, water bottle, book, and anything else you don't absolutely need in the car. (Or see if there's a place you can check these items.) There's a good reason for this: When you're called in, you don't want to be scrambling to gather up a load of stuff, just when you should be extending your hand for a power handshake.

- **Be respectful of the front desk.** The security guard and/or receptionist are important people, too, so be friendly and polite. Be aware that they may be asked what they think of you, so make a good impression.

- **Turn off your cell phone, and put it away before you enter the building.** This means completely *off*, not just on vibrate. Don't read your email or texts in the waiting room or (God forbid!) make phone calls. These behaviors will seriously annoy those in the office and distract you from the important task at hand. Just sit and compose yourself, and try to relax.

■ **Use the restroom.** Go to the restroom *before* you present yourself at the office, if possible. If not, and there's time before the interview, ask the receptionist to direct you to the restroom. There's nothing worse than realizing in the middle of an interview that you really need to relieve yourself.

■ **Check out your surroundings.** As you walk through the building, be sure to take note of the surroundings, the employees, and the general atmosphere. Do you get a good feeling about the place? Do the employees seem to be a lot like you? Do you think you could work here? Remember, *you're* making decisions too!

■ **Relax.** You've prepared yourself thoroughly. Now it's time to relax and focus on being open to whatever happens during the interview. No more memorizing; no more worrying about what to say. It's all there.

Meeting and Greeting—First Impressions

Okay, so you're sitting in the office waiting area, trying to compose yourself, when the door suddenly flies open and your smiling interviewer greets you by name. You rise to meet her, and in just *one-tenth of a second*, she sizes you up and develops a first impression. Yep, it happens that fast. Like that old song says, "Just one look, that's all it took." People make instant judgments about each other. And unfair as those judgments may be, they will definitely affect the outcome of your interview. (We'll talk more about this one-tenth-of-a-second impression in chapter 5.)

Fortunately, thanks to all that advance preparation, you appear polished, confident, and professional. Now, build on this initial positive impression by doing three things:

- **Shake hands with confidence.** You know the drill: Look her straight in the eye, smile, and shake hands like a pro!

- **Smile.** I know I just said you need to smile when shaking hands, but smiling is so important it warrants its own explanation. Studies have shown that others automatically see a smiling person as more intelligent, attractive, relaxed, sincere, and reliable than a person who's not smiling. And that's before a single word has been uttered! Smiling also does some pretty amazing things to your body: It helps decrease the amount of stress-induced hormones circulating through your bloodstream, lowers your blood pressure, and makes you feel more relaxed and happy by stimulating the release of feel-good neurotransmitters in your brain.

  But you're not the only person who reaps benefits from your smile. When others see an attractive, smiling face, the reward centers in their brains become activated, releasing the same feel-good neurotransmitters that are already making you feel so great. In short, each time you smile at someone else, *both of you* will experience activated reward centers and a release of positive chemicals in your brains. No wonder smiling is a great way to establish, maintain, and improve relationships!

- **Walk with self-assurance.** Your carriage reveals a lot about your opinion of yourself. Stand tall, project self-confidence, and walk into a room as if you belong there. Even if you feel nervous, act confident. (Remember what I said before: Behaviors *always* precede feelings. If you want to *feel* self-assured, *act* self-assured.) You are an interesting and talented individual with much to offer! The interviewer will pick up on your poise and confidence and think more highly of you.

Eight Ways to Create the Wrong Impression

We've talked about what you should do to create a great impression. But what about what you *shouldn't* do? Here's a list of things to avoid, as any one of them may be enough to knock you out of the running.

1. *Slamming your former boss or place of work:* Talking trash about others makes you look bad, and the interviewer will wonder what part *you* played in the trouble. He may also wonder what you'll say about him down the road. Always stay positive.

2. *Speaking too softly:* Speaking in a voice that's hard to hear sends the message that you lack confidence— even if you don't. Speak up! You've got significant things to say that others want to hear.

3. *Speaking too loudly:* While speaking up is desirable, projecting as if you're in a football stadium is off-putting and annoying. Make sure others can hear you, but don't leave their ears ringing.

4. *Talking too much:* Telling too many stories or taking a long time to get to the point can make you seem egotistical and/or insecure (not to mention boring). Also, while you're rattling on, you'll be less apt to pick up vital information and clues from the interviewer.

5. *Putting yourself down:* If you act like you don't think much of yourself, why should anyone else think highly of you? Whenever possible, avoid discussing failures, admitting that you're not sure what you want, and responding to questions with, "I don't know."

6. *Repeatedly looking away or looking down while the interviewer is talking to you:* Other people will take your lack of eye contact as a sign that you're not listening, you're bored, or you have no confidence—or maybe all three. Make eye contact.

7. *Cursing or using slang:* Both are unprofessional. If these are your habits, break them before you go on any interviews.

8. *Focusing on your notes:* During an interview, it's fine to refer to notes when asking questions about the company, especially if you have quite a few. But in all other instances, give your full attention to the conversation.

Establishing Rapport

You've probably had the wonderful experience of clicking with another person. Even though you just met, you felt like you'd known her forever, and you were able to open up and be yourself. She seemed to be just like you—a like-minded individual—and you felt understood, listened to, and appreciated. The two of you had what we call rapport—you "got" each other's ideas, feelings, and messages. You automatically liked one another and felt relaxed when you were conversing.

This is exactly what you want to happen when you're talking with the interviewer. If you and she develop rapport—that is, if she recognizes herself in you, realizes the two of you are like-minded, and feels that you understand her—she'll automatically like you and trust you. And you'll be catapulted to the top of her list of job candidates.

Salespeople have long known the importance of establishing rapport before they try to sell a client a product. Sales pros don't begin with, "Look at my product. Isn't it fantastic?" They begin by showing the client that they are just like him, which gains his trust. Once rapport has been established, the client becomes much more open to the presentation or pitch and much more likely to buy.

In the best of all worlds, you and the interviewer will develop a rapport that springs up naturally (and quickly) on its own. But you really can't count on it. Fortunately, there are certain techniques you can use to create rapport in just about any situation.

Look for clues in the office

Recently, a young friend of mine who's a district attorney told me that she had aced just about every interview she had ever had. Surprised, I asked her how, and she replied, "I look around the interviewer's office and pick up clues about what he's interested in and what kind of person he is. Then I tailor my responses to fit." The most obvious example she could think of was the time she saw a coaster bearing the Stella Artois® beer logo sitting on the interviewer's bookshelf.

"Believe it or not," she told me, "one of the interview questions was, 'What's your favorite kind of beer?' It just so happens that I like a lot of different beers, and I actually love Stella Artois, so I said something like, 'Well, it might sound funny because it's kind of obscure, but I really like Stella.' " The interviewer immediately brightened and a rapport was established—and he didn't even realize she'd seen the coaster!

Another young friend of mine walked into an interview, saw a Michigan State University mug on the interviewer's desk, and immediately said, "Oh, wow, did you go to Michigan State?" The interviewer had, and the two of them spent the next 15 minutes talking about their respective college days. Not a bad way to start an interview!

So look around the office for something you might remark on that will excite the interviewer and get him talking—a sports logo coffee cup, a tennis trophy, a travel memento from Mexico, whatever might stimulate a *brief,* positive, opening conversation. If you can, it will definitely work in your favor.

Try mirroring

Mirroring (also called "echoing" or "matching") means reflecting what another person is doing or feeling right now. The simplest description of mirroring is: *Sit like they sit; speak like they speak.* It happens automatically—and often unconsciously—with highly empathic people, and therapists spend years developing this technique to use with their clients. If mirroring is done the right way, the other person (in this case, the interviewer) will unconsciously feel that you and he are similar, that you understand him, and that you are trustworthy.

Mirroring is best done in very understated, simple ways. For example:

- If he is sitting upright in his chair, you sit upright too
- If he lays his hands flat on the table, you might lay your hands flat on the arms of your chair
- If he leans forward, you lean forward

Similarly, you might try matching the interviewer's style of speaking and tone:

- If she speaks quickly, so do you
- If she is excited, you increase the excitement in your own voice
- If she is soft-spoken, serious, measured—or whatever— you are, as well

Here's another way of looking at it: Tune in to what's going on and match it. If the interviewer is serious and subdued, you don't want to be excited and humorous or vice versa. While you certainly shouldn't copy *everything* the interviewer does—if you're too obvious, it may seem like you're mimicking him or that you're being duplicitous—subtly adopting *some* of his postures and gestures will show that the two of you are on the same wavelength.

Engage in active listening

Once you've established rapport, you must build on it. And while the former depends on finding common ground, the latter depends on listening. But just sitting passively while someone talks isn't good enough. You must listen actively in order to build rapport. Active listening is being fully present in the moment and tuning in to the other person's verbal and nonverbal messages in order to understand her meaning.

Here are some tips for becoming a more active listener, especially during your interview:

- **Be courteous and attentive.** Give the interviewer your full attention, and try your best to understand her point of view and what is important to her. Let her finish a complete thought before you jump in and ask questions or make comments.

- **Listen more than you speak.** Be aware that most people (interviewers included) have short attention spans and don't really want to listen to you for more than a few minutes at a time. You'll learn more about the interviewer, the job, and the company by listening. And you'll also make a better impression.

- **Stay engaged while listening.** Don't let your mind wander. Stay focused on the conversation, and show it physically by leaning forward, nodding, and maintaining eye contact.

- **_Ask questions._** When you listen carefully, appropriate questions will naturally come to mind. Use them to clarify what the interviewer has just said. This will show that you're not only interested, but following her train of thought.

- **_Smile._** Smiling is another way of telling other people that you like them and are on board with what they're saying. So smile when it seems appropriate, unless the interviewer herself is non-smiling and dead serious. (Gentle, occasional nodding also helps communicate your involvement in the conversation.)

Active listening is a form of communication in itself and sends strong positive messages like, "I'm with you," "I'm interested," "I'm committed to understanding what you're saying," and "I'm open." When you listen actively, the interviewer will feel heard, understood, and appreciated, making it a great way to strengthen rapport.

Listening Behaviors That Destroy Rapport

Facial expressions, posture, eye contact, and hand gestures can all help build rapport. And they can also destroy it. Since most of the rapport-destroying behaviors are unconscious, it's important that you take a good hard look at your behaviors to ensure you're not doing the following:

- Arranging or fiddling with your hair, jewelry, or clothing

- Checking your watch, cell phone, or other devices

- Doodling
- Rolling your eyes
- Fidgeting or wiggling
- Pointing your finger
- Clenching your fists
- Folding your arms across your chest
- Glaring
- Staring at the ceiling, gazing around the room, looking out the window, or looking anywhere except at the speaker
- Massaging your neck (or anything else)
- Pursing your lips
- Shaking your head "no"
- Shrugging
- Slumping, whether standing or sitting
- Tapping or drumming your fingers, a pen, or a pencil
- Yawning

This list of no-no behaviors may seem totally obvious and hardly worth mentioning. But recently I went to a business meeting with a young man who spent the entire hour absent-mindedly jingling the change in his pocket. (I kept trying to pantomime a "please sit still" message, but he just didn't get it!) Besides being distracting and annoying, the jingling telegraphed an unmistakably negative message:

"I'm bored and can't wait to get out of here." I'm sure he was completely unaware of what he was doing and how others perceived his behavior. Unfortunately, I'm afraid the message got through anyway. Don't be him!

Selling yourself

At this point, the interviewer has seen your résumé and knows how you look, shake hands, talk, smile, and listen. She also has some idea of your personality. What else should you do or say to sell her on the idea of hiring you?

My focus as an interviewer has always been on compatibility rather than competency. It's usually pretty clear whether or not a person can perform a certain job: I just have to look at his résumé and call his references. What I need to find out next is: Will he get along well with our other employees and contribute to a pleasant working environment? As a result, my interviews usually involve lots of chatting in order to get to know the person. And I like to ask questions like, "In the best of all worlds, what would your ideal job be?" or "Are you a morning person or an evening person?" I try to get people to talk so I can get a better sense of them.

But the kinds of interviews you're headed for may not be so laid back. They might be full of tough questions, hypothetical situations, or even unsolvable problems designed to find out how you respond under pressure. How do you ace an interview when you have no idea what they'll throw at you? Here are my suggestions:

- ■ **Breathe, relax, and be yourself.** Remember, your goal is to find the right job match for yourself. And to do that, you need to be authentic. So *don't* pretend you're really interested in a job that you think is less than thrilling. And *don't* act like you love the insurance business when you couldn't care less. Interviewing for a job is kind of like dating. In your dating life, did you ever pretend you were a baseball fan, even though you hated baseball, in order to impress some new love interest? Sooner or later, the truth came out and, naturally, the relationship suffered. The same holds true when you pretend to be what the company wants, rather than who you are. Sooner or later, it will become obvious that you hate accounting or planning meetings or working by yourself, and the job you pretended to be interested in is really wrong for you. Don't misrepresent yourself; it will come back to haunt you.

■ **Remember your USP and the three reasons why the company should hire you.** You worked hard on these before the interview for a reason. At some point, the interviewer will get around to asking what's so special about you, and you can pull them out, like jewels in a treasure chest. Mention just one, with examples, and see if the interviewer wants more. You can also use your USP or one of your three reasons to answer other kinds of questions. For example, if the interviewer asks, "Which work-related accomplishment are you most proud of?" you might say, "Well, I'm an extremely organized person," and go on to give an example, such as, "I started my own charity organization for Sri Lankan tsunami victims when I was 19, and it's still going strong 10 years later." Just don't start reciting your USP or three reasons without being given some kind of opening—it will sound memorized and forced.

■ **Pause when asked a difficult question.** It's perfectly fine to say, "Let me think about that for a moment," or even, "I don't have an answer for that because it hasn't occurred in my life." Difficult questions are often asked not to find out how brilliant you are, but to see how you handle stress. If you can stay calm, you might even be able to change the direction of the interview by saying, "I don't have an answer for that. But may I tell you why I am so interested in getting this job?"

If you can be yourself, stay relaxed, and work in at least a few reasons why the company should hire you, consider yourself a success. Believe me—there are plenty of people who don't get this far!

The successful wrap-up

When all is said and done, what every interviewer really wants to know can be boiled down into four questions:

- Are you really interested in doing this job?
- Are you capable of doing this job?
- Are your values and personality in line with our company culture?
- Will you stay for a reasonable length of time?

Make sure the interviewer knows that your answer to each of these questions is "yes," even if the questions aren't asked. They can make an excellent summary at the end of the interview. When the interviewer asks if you have any questions or anything else you'd like to say, you can respond confidently:

"Yes. I'd just like you to know that I'm really interested in this job. I'm very capable of doing it well. I think I'm a good fit for your company culture. And, if I'm hired, I plan to stay for a very long time and become a valued, reliable team member."

There's not an interviewer alive who won't respond well to this.

After the Interview

Be sure to follow up immediately after the interview with an email thanking the interviewer for seeing you, mentioning something you learned about the job or the company during the interview, and reiterating your interest in the job. It's another chance to put yourself in front of her, plus you'll appear interested, energetic, and efficient. You might also consider sending her a handwritten thank-you note. If you do, make sure it's neat, legible and worded differently from your email. Here comes your name again across the interviewer's desk, this time in an entirely different medium.

The Power of a Handwritten Thank-you Note

When leafing through your daily stack of mail, what's most likely to catch your attention? Not the ads or catalogs. You'll set aside the magazines and save the bills. But a hand-addressed envelope? *That's* the one that you'll open first! Why? Because a hand-addressed envelope is personal and unique—hardly anyone writes anything by hand these days. And if that envelope happens to contain a handwritten note, well, you've really hit the jackpot!

Because handwritten notes take effort and thought, they make their recipients feel special. And since handwriting is a dying art, these notes automatically make an impact. In short, handwritten notes are an excellent way to recognize others and, in the process, become recognized yourself!

When you're winding down after the interview, take some time to reflect on what happened and what you've learned. Make a note of the questions you were asked during the interview, and think about how your responses might be improved. Write down what went well and what you would change. If all of your hard work and preparation pays off and you're offered the job, and if you decide to take it, congratulations! I sincerely hope it fulfills you, opens doors to exciting and challenging new experiences, and provides you with opportunities to grow and prosper.

And if you don't get the job, please remember making it to the interview stage means you're an attractive, viable candidate. Not every interview will (or should) result in a job offer. But each time you're in the hot seat, you'll get better at it, which means you'll be that much closer to landing another job down the line. Next time, you'll have a better idea of the kinds of questions you'll be asked and find it easier to answer them. You'll be more relaxed, sure of yourself, and aware of all that you have to offer. It's called gaining experience.

In the meantime, do whatever you can to improve your skills and make yourself more marketable. Take a training course, work toward a credential, or do volunteer work in your field. As long as you stay focused and positive, you'll eventually succeed—and maybe sooner than you think.

CHAPTER 5

HOW TO FIT IN AND PRESENT A WINNING IMAGE

Congratulations! You've landed a great job and are starting a new adventure. Because you'll be a blank slate to just about everybody you'll meet, this is a golden opportunity to create an image that places you firmly on the path to success. Set yourself apart and become "someone to watch" by making sure that everything you do—how you look, how you act, what you say, what you put in writing, and the quality of your work—is exemplary. People will form opinions of you very quickly, opinions that will be difficult, if not impossible, to change. So decide how you want others to see you (positive, helpful, competent, engaged—you name it), and keep this image in the forefront of your mind at all times.

Cultivating Workplace Relationships

The working world is all about relationships: No one truly works independently, especially if she is part of a company or organization. While some of your relationships will be critical (like the one you have with your boss), those with people who *don't* have power over you can also help or hinder your progress. For example, when you're stuck and need help solving a work-related problem, or you need inside information about how to approach a certain person, or you've been tapped for a committee and must work closely with others, your relationships with your co-workers can be extremely important.

And it may go even further than that. During my tenures at both Crestwood and SkillPath, I could usually tell in advance who was going to quit or be asked to leave simply by observing a disconnect between these employees and their co-workers. It's very rare that someone who's well liked, connected to the team, and supported by others either decides to go (unless she's found a better job) or is kicked out. Thus, having good relationships with your co-workers can be viewed as a kind of career skill that can increase your job longevity, as well.

In short, do your utmost to establish and maintain good relationships with *everyone*—not just with your co-workers, but with top bosses, middle management, assistants, receptionists, custodial and maintenance staff, and everyone else. The more connected you are to the team, the more supported you'll feel, the better you'll perform, the longer you'll stay, and the more fun you'll have.

Set Yourself Apart—but Not Too Much

Here's the dilemma: You want and need to be a part of the team and form solid relationships. But the workplace is competitive, and some of your co-workers will be after the same jobs, titles, and promotions that you want. You need to stand out, but if you're too much of a loner or a Goody-Two-Shoes, your relationships with your co-workers can suffer. So how do you stay friendly with the same people you're competing with?

The best solution is to set yourself apart quietly; that is, become an exemplary employee without showing off. For example:

- Show up 15 minutes early, and leave 15 minutes late every day, without asking for extra pay. If you're on the clock, however, you should clock in and out at the "normal" time.

- Dress *slightly* better than others at your level. (The word "slightly" is key here; otherwise, you'll alienate your co-workers.) Emulate the style of someone you admire who is a level or two above you, but don't wear clothes that make you an outcast.

- Be scrupulous about doing your job correctly, thoroughly, and on time.

- Finish your work early, and ask for more.

- Never get into arguments or altercations with anybody.

- Don't be a tattletale or talk about others behind their backs.

- Don't initiate any office pranks—at least not until you're well established and you fully understand the company culture. Let others act silly and goof around, while you smile and even laugh with them, then continue working.

- Volunteer for jobs that no one else wants to do, and do them without complaint.

- Don't break the rules, even if they seem trivial.

- Ask others to teach you new skills or tasks. You never know what might come in handy.

- Become a safety floor warden; volunteer to train in emergency preparedness; or become the office representative at seminars, meetings, or training sessions. You'll raise your profile and meet more people.

- Forge relationships with people outside of the company whom you meet on the job. They may be the source of a new job one day.

- Stay positive and level-headed, no matter what happens.

Here's the catch: *Never mention to anyone that you're doing these things,* or you may undo all the goodwill you've generated by acting superior or bragging about it. Keep your accomplishments to yourself. I guarantee that eventually people will notice you and be impressed.

Breaking the Ice

So how do you go about establishing these all-important workplace relationships? Let's walk through it step-by-step.

We'll say it's your first day on the job. Someone takes you around the office and introduces you to lots of people, all of whom seem friendly and welcoming. Whenever possible, you jot down their names after meeting them, knowing that nothing is more perishable than the names of strangers. Be aware that the next time you see these people, most will have forgotten your name, who you are, or both. Or they simply may have nothing to say to you. Then it will be up to you to break the ice. The original introduction does this only to a point; you're the one who must get a conversation going if you hope to start a relationship.

I know; you'll probably feel shy and be tempted to hang back. But don't. The sooner you open up the lines of communication, the sooner you can begin connecting. Opportunities to strike up a conversation can crop up in the parking lot, the break room, the elevator, the restroom, or any setting where you come in close contact with others. Dive in and see what transpires!

Here are a few suggestions:

- Smile, look the other person in the eye, and say hello. (It's obvious, but it works.)

- If you haven't met this person before, introduce yourself and ask her name: *"Hi, I'm Josh Brown. I just started working here on Monday. What's your name?"*

- If you have met this person, greet him by name, if possible, and remind him of who you are: *"Oh, hi, Mario. I'm Brooke Goldstein. I met you the other day when I started my new job in HR."*

- Give the other person a *sincere* compliment, and follow it up with an open-ended question. (An open-ended question is one that can't be answered with a simple "yes" or "no."): *"That's a fantastic purse. Where did you find it?"*

- Make a lighthearted comment: *"I can't believe how cold it's been lately."*

- Try to engage the other person by asking an open-ended question that's not too personal: *"Why do you think the parking lot was so full today?"*

The purpose of these icebreakers is simply to get the other person talking. That's because the more a person talks to you, the more likely he is to think well of you, let down his defenses, and deepen the relationship—which is exactly what you want. Just be sure to keep the tone light, and avoid questions that pry into his personal life or push views that may seem controversial. Then tune in to his response. If he feels like talking to you, he'll jump in and take the lead. But if he seems uninterested, busy, or closed off for any reason, let him go. Above all else, you don't want to be seen as a pest.

It takes time and repeated exposure to others to build relationships, so be patient. You'll find out soon enough who is interested in getting to know you and taking the conversation to a deeper level and who isn't. But no matter how you're received, continue to smile and greet people whenever you encounter them, even those you don't know.

Building a Powerful and Positive Professional Image

Like every other human being, you are constantly sending messages about yourself that reveal your thoughts, feelings, attitudes, values, and desires. And most of these messages don't take the form of words! Your facial expression, eye contact, posture, gestures, vocal tone, and vocal volume communicate as much, or more, than the actual words you use. They can enhance or undermine your overall message and improve or damage your professional image. The scary thing is, you probably don't even realize which messages you're sending! So let's take a look at the seven ways we communicate, and the roles each plays in creating a professional image.

1. Facial expression

Perhaps the most important part of your image is the expression you wear on your face. As I've already mentioned, the newest research shows that when we first meet one another, we make a *one-tenth-of-a-second* judgment about whether we're going to like the other person—literally less than one second! (There's another, more measured judgment that takes a little while longer—usually a couple of minutes—but that first one tends to stick like glue, no matter what follows.) This research tells me that the under-one-second judgment cannot possibly be based upon anything other than what your face is saying. So what should you aim for? Upon initial contact with a new person, a neutral-to-positive facial expression is the most powerful image you can present. By "neutral," I mean your emotions are *not* on display—you don't look thrilled, angry, confused, or anything else. And by "neutral-to-positive," I mean that you want to skew the neutral slightly toward the positive— strive to appear open and approachable, with a friendly demeanor and a slight smile. (A huge smile can seem artificial or just plain strange.) It's important to keep your emotions to yourself (especially negative emotions) so you're in charge of what you reveal. Do your best to avoid scowling, pressing your lips together, rolling your eyes, or looking bored, no matter how you may feel.

In a nutshell: **Keep it neutral-to-positive.**

2. Eye contact

You've probably had the disconcerting experience of talking to someone who won't make eye contact with you. It's easy to jump to the conclusion that she's hiding something, lying, or simply doesn't like you. While it might have been due to shyness or thinking about what she wanted to say next, her lack of eye contact made you feel uncomfortable or even suspicious. To avoid falling into this trap, be sure to look people in the eye when communicating—that is, to a point.

Yes, there is such a thing as too much eye contact! In general conversation, it's considered impolite (or weird) to stare steadily at the other person for several minutes without breaking eye contact.

Only two types of people do this: Hostile/aggressive types and lovers! So go ahead and make eye contact for a few seconds, and then break it for a brief moment—look aside and gather your thoughts, and then look back at the other person. You don't want to give him the feeling that you're trying to stare him down (or that you're madly in love!).

In a nutshell: **Make it (mostly) and break it (just a little).**

3. Posture

The most powerful way to position yourself physically is to look broad and stable. With your head and body facing straight ahead, you stand with your feet slightly apart, weight evenly distributed, and shoulders back and down (not hunched). Your hands are at your sides or in some kind of comfortable position. You're as tall and wide as you can make yourself, which allows you to summon as much power as possible.

When I was a child, I was taught to stand in "model's pose," especially for photos. You position your feet at 10 and 12 on an imaginary clock, and turn your body toward the camera at a three-quarter angle. "Model's pose" supposedly showed off the nicest, most slender lines of the body. However, it is *not* a powerful stance. If anything, it minimizes a person. If I were a banker standing in model's pose while trying to convince you to invest in my bank, would you be sold? I think not. You'd probably wonder how I escaped from the nearest department store fashion show!

I know that completely changing your posture sounds like a tall order (no pun intended). For example, if you're a woman and you happen to be a little self-conscious about your chest, you might find it hard to start walking around with your shoulders pulled back. So, to start with, try putting your hands into your pockets. It's not quite the powerful stance you're aiming for, but it will bring your shoulders back naturally. Eventually you can begin to leave a hand out. And down the line you can leave the other hand out. (We behavioral psychologists call this "successive approximation"— doing something one step at a time until you've accomplished the entire task or behavior.) By taking a gradual approach, you can get there. Just don't do it overnight or you'll end up feeling (and looking) awkward.

As for sitting posture, here's a special note for women. You may have been taught to sit with your legs (or at least your ankles) crossed. Unfortunately, this makes you slouch and lean forward a little bit, which sends the wrong message. If I sat in a board of directors meeting like that, here's the message I'd be telegraphing to everyone in the room: "I don't take up a lot of space, so is it okay if I stay here?" Or, "Can I just sit here for a while if I don't bother any of you?"

Instead, whether you're a man or a woman, use your body language to claim your space. Walk in the room and sit down as if you have a right to be there. Sit tall, be broad, and physically send this message: "Here I am. I am this big and no smaller. I have a presence." If you want to cross your legs because it feels more comfortable, go ahead. But be sure to pull your shoulders back and sit up in your chair—don't slouch or hunch your shoulders.

In a nutshell: **Stand tall; be broad.**

4. Hands

It's natural to use your hands while you're talking. And if your hand gestures match your message, they can illustrate a point, express a feeling, or help your listener visualize something. *Not* using your hands at all can make you seem indifferent or disengaged, even robotic, and you certainly don't want that. But if you use your hands too much, or make gestures that are big or wild, they can distract the listener from your message. You can see this clearly on television when the camera comes in for a tight shot of a person's face and upper torso. If her hands are flailing around, that's all you can see, which is why newscasters are constantly told to keep their hands still and completely away from their faces. Fortunately, we in the real world don't have to (and shouldn't) act like newscasters. So go ahead and use your hands in any way that feels natural. Just don't overdo it.

However, there are a few caveats: First, keep your hands away from your face. Repeatedly touching your face or your hair can be distracting and annoying to your listeners. Men with beards often have a habit of stroking their chins; women with sideswept bangs may constantly flick their hair back from their faces. Some people also touch their fingers to their lips or chin, which makes them look unsure of themselves. Others like to prop up their chins with their hands when sitting, which can make them seem tired, bored, or disengaged. If any of these are your habits, do your best to break them.

Second, make a conscious effort to relax your hands, fold them, or let them lie on a table or in your lap when you're conversing with others. It's easy to engage in nervous habits like fidgeting, doodling, jingling keys (remember my story about the young man who jingled his way through an entire meeting?), clenching, massaging yourself, or tapping your fingers or a pen. All of these can signal nervousness, boredom, impatience, and/or negativity—not the messages you want to send.

Finally (this should go without saying but I'll say it anyway), don't rip your fingernails, pick at your cuticles, or otherwise misuse your hands, especially in front of others. It can totally ruin the self-confident, relaxed, in-control image that you're striving to project. Leave your poor hands alone.

In a nutshell: **Use them, but not too much.**

What Message Is Your Body Sending?

We all constantly send messages about ourselves via our body language. What is your body saying? Tune in; then substitute positive messages for the negative ones.

Negative Body Language

- Slouching, sinking into chairs
- Fidgeting with a pencil/doodling
- Crossing your legs and swinging your foot
- Folding your arms across your chest (or other "closed" postures)
- Pulling your chin down
- Not making eye contact
- Tilting your head to one side

Message sent: *"I'm unsure of myself, nervous, disengaged, and closed."*

Positive Body Language

- Head up
- Hands at sides, or on lap, fists unclenched
- Direct eye contact
- Standing straight with shoulders back
- Weight distributed evenly on feet

■ Sitting straight and leaning forward slightly to show interest

Message sent: *"I'm confident, intelligent, capable, and in charge."*

5. Vocal tone

The tone of your voice—that is, its quality and the emotions it conveys—always sends a stronger message than your words. Every time you open your mouth, your tone will reveal whether you're confident, assured, uncertain, bored, annoyed, stressed-out, enthusiastic, skeptical, or a million other states of being. Just imagine a person who has been insulted and turns on the perpetrator with a sarcastic or even furious, "I'm *sorry*?" Anyone within earshot knows darned well that she's not the least bit sorry. What she's really saying is, "How dare you say that to me?" Her tone makes that absolutely clear, regardless of the words she's chosen. Much of your vocal tone is the result of intonation, the rise and fall of your vocal pitch, or the "melody" of speech. Different pitches within a phrase form patterns that we recognize as statements, requests, and questions, and these patterns characterize your speech.

■ **Statements usually begin at a higher pitch and end on a lower one.** These are declarations, plain and simple (e.g., "I set off for the grocery store and ended up at the mall."). By the time you reach the word "mall," your voice is probably at a lower (if not much lower) pitch than it was when you started the sentence.

■ **Requests typically maintain the same pitch throughout.** While phrased as questions, these are really instructions or orders, and the vocal pitch stays on an even keel (e.g., "Can you bring me the Purchases file, please.").

■ *Questions usually start at a lower pitch and end on a higher one.* These are designed to elicit information and end on a higher pitch, implying the need for some form of resolution (e.g., "Is that really what you want?").

These are the standard pitch patterns, but not everyone adheres to them. And that can get in the way of communicating in a clear and powerful manner. One power-sapping intonation pattern that many people (especially young people) have adopted is upspeak, the tendency to make statements or requests sound like questions. In other words, the vocal inflections go *up* at the end of the sentence, as if asking a question, instead of going down in pitch or staying on an even keel. You've heard this pattern so often that you may not even notice it, as in:

> *"So I was on my way to a meeting? And then I stopped at a red light? And then in my rearview mirror I saw a cop come up behind me. So I reached over and grabbed my wallet? And then I pulled out my ID? And for some reason, he, like, just drove off? Unbelievable!"*

My theory about the rising pitch at the end of a statement is that it's actually a bit of shorthand. Instead of saying, "Are you following me?" or "Do you agree?" the speaker folds the question into his statement by going up in pitch at the end. Then he looks for some kind of signal that, yes, the listener's on board and agrees. This way, he doesn't have to stop his story to ask for and receive this verification.

Unfortunately, this habit can easily become a dominant speech pattern, and it runs counter to the powerful, self-assured image you're trying to convey. In fact, it practically screams self-doubt. Making statements that sound like questions sends the message that you're unsure of yourself and what you're saying, that you don't know if you're making sense or will be understood. If you use this tone in a business meeting or when making a presentation, you'll definitely sound like you don't know what you're talking about.

So make your statements sound like statements rather than questions. Bring your pitch down at the end of your sentences, or keep the pitch even if you're making a request. Go up in pitch only if you're truly asking a question.

In a nutshell: **Keep your voice in its lower register, and watch the use of your vocal pitch.**

Ladies: Squealing Diminishes Power!

We women, with our musical, up-and-down vocal quality, use something called a "widely varying intonational pitch pattern." Pretty fancy, huh? It means that we have four pitch patterns, while men only have three. We use this extra high pitch to express delight, surprise, or excitement, as in, *"I didn't know you were going to be here today!"* We may also use it to talk to babies, small children, and pets (as an aside, many men do the same thing when talking to these same three groups). But we never use it indiscriminately. You won't hear anyone walk into the dry cleaners and screech, *"Hi! Are my clothes ready?!"*

While women have an extra way to communicate through intonation that's unique to our sex, this fourth pitch pattern is the one that takes away our power. So if you want to be taken seriously and be seen as a powerful communicator, you'll need to jettison this high-pitched voice, and stick to the lower registers.

It can be tough to eliminate the fourth pattern completely.

I must admit I still sometimes answer the phone, "This is Denise; may I help you?" and then suddenly exclaim, "*Hey!*" using a much higher pitch. If I don't know in advance who's on the line and it turns out to be someone I like, my surprise just naturally sends my voice upward. But just as quickly, I always bring it back down to a lower pitch. In general, I try to use the fourth pitch pattern only when I'm in social situations or out having fun.

6. Vocal volume

Your voice should be exactly as loud as it needs to be for your listeners to hear you, whether you're talking to one person or 2,500. If your voice is too soft, your listeners will strain to hear you and may think you lack conviction, don't have your facts straight, or aren't ready to present your message. They may also become weary or irritated and simply tune you out. So to project a powerful image, you must project your voice. And guess what? Even if you think you have a naturally soft or quiet voice, it *is* a very powerful, muscular instrument, capable of being heard at great distances. Your vocal chords can actually carry your voice, unaided, throughout the largest of concert halls—just ask any opera singer. You simply might need a little practice and encouragement to find your innate vocal strength. That being said, you don't want to break anybody's eardrums with your speaking voice or come across as too loud and forceful.

In a nutshell: **Speak up, but not too loudly.**

Thinking About Working on Your Voice?

Just about anyone can benefit from a few visits to a vocal coach. He or she can help you find your "real voice" (which is probably about half an octave lower than you think) and improve your vocal volume and quality. Articulation, enunciation, and diction can also be addressed, if necessary. Your voice and manner of speaking are crucial parts of your image: Think about investing a little time and money in improving them!

7. Verbal content

Words are just one of the seven parts of communication, but they're special because they are the major conveyors of *ideas*. And you can fortify both your words and your professional image by communicating assertively. Assertive communication means expressing yourself effectively and standing up for your own beliefs and rights, while simultaneously respecting the beliefs and rights of others. This is an extremely important concept, and I'm not exaggerating when I say it's *essential* to your success. We'll talk more about it in chapter 7, but for now, let's just say that assertive communication is saying what you mean and meaning what you say, without discounting or disparaging anyone else. You're not a doormat, but you're also not a bully. You're not pretending to agree, then saying "no" with your actions. You're clear about where you stand, while being respectful of others and their views. Being assertive will help increase your self-esteem, lower your stress level, earn you the respect of others, and ensure excellent communication.

Here are a few tips that will help you communicate more assertively and clearly:

- **Use "I" statements.** Phrasing your statements in the first person ("I feel … " "I think … " "I disagree … ") is less accusatory and more factual than using "you" statements ("You said … " "You think … " "You want … ").

- **Keep your responses short.** Get to the point, explain *one* idea, and allow the other person to respond. Going on and on or addressing several ideas at once is overwhelming and confusing for your listeners. You run the risk of being misunderstood or being tuned out altogether.

- **Slow down your rate of speaking.** Talking too fast can make you seem nervous, uncertain, or aggressive and can tire your listener and turn her off. A brief, moderately paced answer is more likely to be digested and accepted.

- **Sort your emotions from your thoughts.** Becoming emotionally attached to your thoughts or ideas gets in the way of clear communication, especially when you're trying to resolve a conflict. You certainly don't want to fly off the handle or start crying. To keep your emotions under control, take some deep breaths, wait a while if possible, and focus on your ideas rather than your feelings.

You'll find a more in-depth discussion in chapter 7 because there's a great deal more to assertive communication than these four tips, but they're a good place to start.

In a nutshell: **Be assertive.**

Avoid mixed messages

The first four methods of communication (facial expression, eye contact, posture, and hands) are visual, while the last three (vocal tone, vocal volume, and verbal content) are auditory. But whether seen or heard, if one of those components doesn't blend with the others, your listener will receive a "mixed message." For example, let's say a co-worker is telling you how much she likes her boss, while simultaneously shaking her head "no" and looking dispirited. Or a new acquaintance is saying, "I'm so excited to meet you," while offering a very weak, noncommittal handshake and avoiding eye contact. In each case, you feel that something is not right. The same will be true for your listeners if you send mixed messages. And here's something interesting: Numerous studies confirm that when a person's words don't match how she looks (her facial expression, eye contact, and body language), we as listeners will go with what we see over what we hear 100 percent of the time! That's why it's essential for you to *look* like you mean what you're saying. If you don't, your message will be overridden by your visual presentation.

A good communicator says the same thing all seven ways. There are no mixed messages. Make sure you do the same.

One Last Thing ...

Your personal image and your professional relationships should be two of your most prized possessions: Either one can make or break your career. So build them carefully and thoughtfully, treat them like gold, and guard them with everything you've got.

In the process, be as *genuinely* friendly, kind, and helpful as you can to everyone you come in contact with in the business world. (Need I mention that the same holds true in the rest of the world as well?) This includes your co-workers, even if you're competing for the same job or promotion, and people who may never be in a position to help you get ahead. Not only is it the right thing to do as a human being, but if you're well liked and seen as a truly nice person, you'll reap rewards down the road.

Some of your co-workers will eventually rise through the ranks, either at your company or a different one, and may be able to help you. Some may end up working for you (or you may end up working for them!), and if they like you, they will have your back. And others may simply be part of the company culture, greeting you in the hallway and waving at you in the parking lot. No matter where these people land, those who think well of you can make your life easier and more pleasant. For all of these reasons and more, be nice to everyone you meet.

CHAPTER 6

WORKPLACE ETIQUETTE AND COMMON COURTESY

Let's face it—you're going to be spending more time with your co-workers than just about anybody else in your life. So it makes sense, personally and professionally, to keep things running as smoothly as possible by observing the rules of common courtesy. Unfortunately, common courtesy isn't all that common these days. According to one study, 8 out of 10 Americans believe a lack of courtesy and respect is "a major problem," and 6 out of 10 think the problem is only getting worse. Surprisingly, almost half of them also confessed that their *own* rude behavior and lack of etiquette was contributing to the problem. Could you be one of those people? Let's take a look.

15 Sure-fire Ways to Drive Your Co-workers Crazy!

The lack of courtesy is every bit as common in the business environment as it is elsewhere. And even people who might otherwise be considered "nice" and "polite" commit their share of faux pas. So what is it that's driving everybody nuts at the office? MJN Consulting surveyed 500 office professionals and came up with a list of 10 common workplace discourtesies. To this list, I added five of my own, coming up with 15 ways to ratchet up everybody's stress levels and make yourself really unpopular. If that's your aim, just do the following:

1. Take a long time to respond to phone calls, voice mails, or emails (or, better yet, don't respond at all).

2. Use the last piece of paper in the copier and leave it empty.

3. At meetings, show disrespect for everyone by arriving late, leaving your cell phone in ringing mode, answering your phone in the middle of the meeting, or checking your messages.

4. Make a mess in the microwave, and leave it for someone else to clean up.

5. Program the copy machine to use special features, and leave it that way for the next person.

6. Cruise the office looking for people to chat with instead of working.

7. Send your co-workers long email messages, jokes, or downloads.

8. "Borrow" office supplies from your co-workers, then forget (or neglect) to replace them.

9. Take the last cup of coffee and leave the pot empty. (Extra points if it burns!)

10. Play music or videos on your computer loud enough so others hear it.

And now for my own personal non-favorites:

11. Blab endlessly (and loudly) about your personal life to any co-worker who will listen. Then call your friends and tell the same stories all over again, so everyone in the office has to hear them multiple times.

12. Come to work sick and spread your germs around.

13. Wear enough cologne so your co-workers can smell you halfway down the hall.

14. Chew gum noisily. Even better, blow bubbles and pop them.

15. Smell up the entire office by cooking fish or broccoli in the microwave or burning toast or popcorn.

I'm sure you'll be able to come up with a few of your own once you've been on the job for a while. But you get the idea. If you *don't* want to be an office nuisance, steer clear of these behaviors!

Workplace Etiquette—the Basics

You may think of etiquette as a fancy, complex set of rules that you have to master in order to avoid stepping on other people's toes. But it's really just common sense based on a very simple idea, summed up this way: *Your actions affect others, regardless of your intent.* So courtesy and respect for others should always be at the top of your agenda. This is particularly true in an office, where people are concentrated in a small space for long hours, day in and day out. In such an environment, even small things like talking too loudly or leaving a mess in the kitchen can really rankle others, especially if they occur repeatedly.

The rules of office etiquette could probably fill an entire book. But two of them top the list in importance: Keep the noise down and respect and recognize others. If you observe only these two rules, your office etiquette will be up to snuff.

Keep the noise down

Employees in an office environment are a captive audience, which means that whatever one person does or says will be seen and heard by just about everybody else. Multiply this by the number of people in your office, and you've got an environment that's just brimming with noise. There are people talking, laughing, and (sometimes) yelling; phones ringing; copiers grinding; microwaves beeping; and maybe even outdoor noises coming in through the windows, like street traffic or planes taking off.

Besides being annoying, noise is tough on your body and your brain. Noise raises your blood pressure and ramps up your sympathetic nervous system, which prompts your body to pump out fight-or-flight hormones like adrenaline and cortisol. Your stress level rises, setting your body and brain on edge. Then there's the irritation and frustration of having to work harder to concentrate. You can see why tempers get short and productivity goes down when there's too much noise in the office.

You probably think that you, personally, don't make a lot of noise and that everyone in the area *doesn't* hear your phone in speaker mode, your music, or your recap of what you did last night. But believe me, they do. Even if they can't quite make out what you're saying, your noise is enough to distract and irritate them. So be a good office mate and tamp down your share of the racket by following these guidelines:

- **Lower your voice.** Keep it down, especially during personal conversations. Raucous laughter can be especially annoying, so modulate it. (Plus, nobody likes to be left out of a good joke!)

- **Be discreet.** Confine long chats with your co-workers to the coffee room or lunchtime, or arrange to get together after work.

- **Aim for privacy whenever you're on the phone.** Stay off the speakerphone. Make personal phone calls on your break, after hours, or away from others. And if you're lucky enough to have an office, close the door when you're on the phone.

- **Use earphones.** This is really the only way to go if you want to play music or listen to anything on your computer.

- **Use the intercom or instant messaging to communicate with co-workers.** Shouting back and forth is really disruptive, and there's no reason for it with today's technology.

- **Mute your cell phone while in the office.** There's no reason to bother everyone with your post-dubstep ringtone when you can put it on vibrate or silent.

- **Close the door to the copy room.** Copy machines are really noisy. Do everyone a favor and close the door when you're making copies.

- **Refrain from chewing gum and, especially, popping bubbles.** Both are noisy and considered major faux pas in the business world.

A quiet, peaceful workplace is ideal for everybody, both physically and psychologically. Do your part to keep it that way!

Respect and recognize others

At this point in your life, you've probably already held down a few jobs, even if they've been only minor positions, like the one I had selling snow cones in a ballpark. So take a moment and think back on your work experiences. What did you like? What did you *not* like? Who did you appreciate, and what did they do (or not do) that made you feel good about yourself? Next, narrow it down to your very favorite past work experience. What was so special about it? My guess is that you're remembering a time when you felt valued. Most likely, it was a specific *someone* (or several someones) who made you feel worthwhile. You felt important, noticed, and appreciated for your contributions, no matter what your specific job happened to be. You felt like you were *respected and recognized*.

Nearly everyone wants to be treated with respect and recognized as an individual with special attributes. And you can give your co-workers these wonderful gifts by doing the following:

- **Say "hello" and smile at everyone you see.** This applies whether you know the person or not.

- **Say "please" and "thank you."** Always; every time you ask for or receive anything.

- **Say "good night" or "good-bye" at the end of the day.** Don't just slink away.

- **Open doors for others.** It doesn't matter which gender; hold the door if you get there first.

- **Introduce yourself if you don't know someone.** Don't wait to be approached; you may wait forever.

- **Look at people when they talk to you.** When someone is talking with you, stop what you're doing and give him your undivided attention. Don't look over his shoulder, watch others walk by, or continue to tap away at your keyboard.

- *Learn people's names right away, and use them.* This will show that you recognize and respect them as individuals.

- *Address people by their preferred names.* Don't make up nicknames or arbitrarily shorten a person's name without permission (e.g., Sue for Susan, Tony for Antonio).

- *Take care to spell names correctly.* People feel disrespected and annoyed when their names are misspelled.

- *Learn a few facts about each person and ask polite, friendly questions.* But ask questions only if and when it seems appropriate. And never ask prying, nosy questions.

- *Give others* genuine *compliments.* Do this as often as possible; people never tire of being appreciated and admired. But make sure your compliments are always sincere.

- *Return phone calls, emails, and other messages as soon as you receive them.* You might say nothing more than, "I'll get back to you as soon as I have an answer," but at least you're not leaving others hanging.

- *Respect others' personal space.* Knock before entering someone's office, or if the door is open, catch that person's eye and ask, "Do you have a minute?" Wait to be asked in, and don't sit down unless you're invited. Similarly, don't enter another person's cubicle without an invitation.

- *Respect others' time and privacy.* Keep your interruptions of others to a minimum, and apologize if you're intruding on another activity or disturbing their concentration.

- *Respect others' possessions.* Don't grab a pen or an interoffice envelope off someone else's desk without permission. Don't "borrow" supplies without asking. And don't help yourself to others' food from the office refrigerator, unless you've been invited.

- *Be careful about eating at your desk.* In some offices this is considered okay; in others the noise and smells can be disruptive. Look around or ask what's generally accepted before you dive into that fragrant chili cheese dog with extra onions while continuing to work.

- *Cough or sneeze into a tissue or your own sleeve.* Never cough or sneeze into the air or in anyone's direction. Afterward, say, "Excuse me," and go wash your hands. And if you're actually sick, stay home. No one wants to catch your cold or flu.

- *If someone else sneezes, it's considered polite to say something.* "Bless you" or "gesundheit" (which literally means "health") are commonly said. Observe what's typically done in your office and follow suit.

- *Don't wear perfume or cologne to the office.* You're sharing a small space with other people. Some may be allergic to perfume or cologne, and others may be annoyed when forced to smell it. Better to leave it off.

Email Etiquette

Email is fast and efficient and doesn't require postage or laboriously typed letters on fancy letterhead. But it's definitely got its downsides. For one thing, like all written communication, it lacks *six* of the seven components of communication: Facial expression, eye contact, posture, hand gestures, vocal tone, and vocal volume. This means you're relying completely on verbal content to get your message across. No one will be able to tell by the twinkle in your eye that you're kidding. Or see by your body language that you're open to discussion. So you'll need to be especially careful about what you say in your emails, or you may be misunderstood. And because it's so easy just to dash off a few words and hit "send," plenty of mistakes can slip through, feelings can get hurt, and mis-understandings can occur. So slow down, think about what you're saying and how it might be received, and follow these general rules of email etiquette:

- **Reply promptly.** Emails should be responded to in less than 24 hours; however, people within your company will probably expect you to get back to them right away.

- **Use a salutation.** Don't just launch into your message; it's too abrupt and cold (and "being too busy" is not a legit-imate excuse for poor manners). Begin your emails with the recipient's name preceded by "Hello," "Good morning," or "Hi." With more formal emails, address the person as you would in a business letter ("Dear Ms. Chan"). After this initial email, if you continue with a back-and-forth exchange, you can leave off the salutation and go directly to your response—it becomes more like a live conversation (i.e., you don't need to say "Hi, John" each time).

- **Use the subject line.** Clearly indicate the topic of your email in the subject line, using a few words that directly relate to what you've written. A clearly stated subject will make your email less likely to be overlooked and easier for the receiver to find and file.

- **Be careful of the tone.** Emails take on a tone based on the words you've chosen, so try to use the most neutral language possible, while still getting the point across. Joking and sarcasm can be dangerous without accompanying body lan-guage, so be careful. Always reread what you've written with a critical eye to see if it might possibly be misunderstood. If so, rewrite it.

- **Use correct grammar and spelling.** Unlike the emails you might dash off to your sister, business emails need complete sentences, good grammar, and correct spelling. Although email is usually less formal than a business letter, its content should reflect the fact that you're a well-educated, professional person.

- **Use completely spelled-out words.** This should go without saying, but unless it's completely accepted in your company culture, don't use text lingo like "U," "4," or "BTW." Save it for your buds.

- **Skip the emoticons, colors, and fancy fonts.** Not only are these distracting, but they can make you look immature and unprofessional.

- **Don't use all caps.** Putting words or entire sentences in capital letters within a paragraph makes it look like you're screaming at the reader. Bolding, italicizing, or underlining can have the same effect. Leave them out of your business emails, unless they're part of an outline structure.

- **Be careful what you put in print.** Never say *anything* in an email that you wouldn't want others to read or hear. All it takes to spread your email around is a click of the "forward" button. Similarly, I've witnessed several embarrassing email faux pas when someone accidentally hit the "reply all" button when he meant to send a secret (and sarcastic) aside to only *one* person in the email group. Talk about an "oops!"

- **Use a sign-off.** Close your email with "Thanks," "Best regards," or "Sincerely," depending on the level of formality. And add your name.

- **Proofread your emails before sending.** Emails count. Read and reread each one before sending it to check for misspellings, poor grammar, missing words, and so on. Does it say what you've intended? Is your message clear, or is it ambiguous? Make sure your email is letter-perfect before it goes out. Remember, everything you say and do reflects who you are.

Posting About Your Job (or Your Boss) on Social Media

Remember back in chapter 3 when we talked about erasing anything you wouldn't want a prospective employer to see on your Facebook® profile, Twitter® feed, LinkedIn® page, or other social networking sites *before* you sent out your résumé? Well, keeping a positive presence online continues to be important after you've landed a job—and on into the future.

When you've had a bad day at work, you may be tempted to hop on Facebook and vent, but *don't*. It can easily get back to your current boss, co-workers, the company's top executives, and plenty of other people you probably hadn't considered. Your potential future employers may find it, too, even after you've deleted it. (It may be traceable.) In short, don't post anything you wouldn't want your mother or your boss to read. And never post *anything* when you're overly tired, angry, upset, high, or intoxicated. It's just not worth it.

Phone Etiquette

Even in our age of almost constant electronic communication, there are still plenty of phone calls being made. One big advantage of phone calls is the addition of your voice, enhancing communication with your vocal tone and volume. Your voice can often project facial expression as well—we've all "heard" a smile over the phone. Another advantage is you can get immediate feedback about what you're saying, so you can explain if necessary. Phone calls are always more personal than emails, so if you want to add that human touch and you can't pay a visit, a phone call is the next best thing. Still, definite rules govern business conversations on the phone, so make sure you always do the following:

If you're the one placing the call

- **Greet the person who answers the phone and identify yourself.** No matter who picks up the phone, greet that person cordially by saying, "hello," "good morning," "good afternoon," or something similar. Then clearly state your first and last name, as in, "This is Natalie Jablonski." Don't try to be friendly by launching into "Hi, how are you doing today?" before you tell the other person who you are. She will be suspicious of you and wonder what you're after.

- **Immediately state your reason for calling.** Don't beat around the bush, make jokes, or try to get friendly with whoever answered the phone. Get to the point. If you're calling for a specific person, politely ask to speak to that person, as in, "I'd like to speak with Robert Hernandez, please." If you need to talk to someone but you don't know her name, say, "I need to speak with the person who's in charge of public relations. Can you direct me?" Or if you need some kind of service, say, "I'm having trouble with my copy machine. Can you tell me who to speak to?"

- **Say "thank you."** Once the person who answered the phone answers your question or says she is about to connect you to someone else, thank her.

- **Identify yourself again, if necessary.** When you've been connected with another party, unless that person picks up the phone and greets you by name, identify yourself again, as in, "Hi, Jessica. This is Natalie Jablonski." If Jessica happens to be someone you know well, you might leave off your last name so you don't sound too formal. Then wait for Jessica to respond so you can be sure she knows it's you.

- **Take the other person's cue on personal chitchat.** If she greets you enthusiastically and asks you about your weekend, go ahead and have a short friendly chat (if you can spare the time). But if she responds with a quick, "Hi, Natalie. What can I do for you?" get to the point and finish the phone call as soon as you can.

If you're the one receiving the call

Protocol for receiving a phone call varies according to how elevated your position is: If you're a warehouse clerk, you'll do certain things differently than if you're a CEO. But in general, phone etiquette is much the same.

- **When picking up a call, say "hello" and/or identify yourself.** If you're answering your own phone, the person who is calling already knows who you are, so you can simply say, "Hello." (However, I always say, "Hello. This is Denise," because sometimes calls can be accidentally misdirected.) But if you're answering for a whole department or you're one of three staff members answering the same phone, you'll need to give the name of the department and your own name, as in, "Shipping Department, this is Brittany Cohen speaking."

- **Respond to the caller with some kind of greeting.** Once the caller identifies herself, it's polite to say, "Hello, Sabrina. How can I help you?" Or, if you know Sabrina, you might want to say something more friendly, like, "Hi, Sabrina. What's up on your end?"

- **Don't leave callers on hold for more than a minute or two.** If you're on the phone and another call comes in that you need to take, ask the first caller if you can put her on hold. If she agrees, don't leave her on hold for more than two minutes, max—and preferably a lot less. If you can't resume the call by then, ask if you can call her back. Then follow through and do it!

For both callers and receivers

Everyone should be sure to do the following:

- **Be cordial.** Do your utmost to be pleasant and make problem solving your priority. If you smile when you're speaking, the other person will sense it and feel more at ease.

- **Ask before you put the other party on speakerphone.** Speakerphone should be used only for calls that involve several people who are gathered in the same place to use one phone. Using speakerphone for any other reason makes it seem like you're so disinterested you can't be bothered to pick up your phone receiver. (There's actually one other condition: When you need both hands free to type notes about the conversation you're having, in which case, it's polite to let the person know your reasons for using speakerphone.)

- **Sign off.** At the end of the call, say something pleasant like, "It was nice talking with you," or "Great, we've got that solved," or "I'm looking forward to our lunch next week." And always thank the other person, even if you're the one doing the favor, making the plan, or resolving the issue.

- **Say "good-bye."** Everyone deserves a "hello" at the beginning of every transaction and a "good-bye" at the end, whether it's a meeting or a phone call. "Okay" (click) just doesn't cut it. In the movies, people are always barking out orders over the phone, then hanging up abruptly, but it's just plain rude. Don't do it—even if Tom Cruise does! (After all, we have to forgive him because he's probably busy saving the world from aliens.)

- ■ ***Personalize your voice mail.*** Record a pleasant voice mail message in your own voice so people will know that it's you and they've dialed the right number. A robotic recitation of your number is off-putting.

Meeting Etiquette

Whether you work in sales, health care, construction, a government job— you name it—it's almost a sure thing that you're going to end up in a meeting or two (or more likely, lots of them) during your career. Never is your professional image on display more than during meetings, so be sure to follow these basic rules to make the best impression.

- ■ ***Be on time.*** For meetings, "on time" means arriving five minutes early; for interviews, it's 10 minutes early. Don't arrive any earlier for either of them! There may be a prep meeting still in progress that you aren't privy to. Or your presence may simply make others nervous. At the same time, don't be late. If you've been held up, try to let someone know why, where you are, and how soon you'll be there.

- ■ ***Dress properly.*** Wear whatever is considered appropriate for your position and your company. This is not the time to get wild or creative, unless you happen to be working in fields that encourage it.

- ■ ***Be courteous, pleasant, and positive.*** Be on your best behavior, and show consideration for others' ideas, thoughts, and feelings.

- ■ ***Turn off your cell phone.*** Don't check your email or messages or even look at your phone during meetings. It's rude to everyone involved and sends the message that you're not interested in what's happening at the moment. If you happen to be in the middle of a true emergency and absolutely must be available, briefly tell others your situation, set your phone to vibrate, and glance at incoming messages only fleetingly.

■ **Be prepared.** If you are slated to give a presentation, make sure your input is organized, concise, and on point. Avoid digressing or rattling on.

■ **Be a team player.** Be concerned with others, not just yourself. Listen and try hard to understand their points of view. Be open to the possibility that your point of view might be incomplete, or possibly even wrong. Compromise whenever possible.

■ **Don't interrupt others.** Let other people finish their thoughts and explain themselves completely before you jump in.

■ **Don't dominate the meeting.** It's good to contribute if you have something relevant and valuable to say. But don't contribute too much. Let the chairperson lead the meeting, and allow others to give input.

■ **In case of conflict, don't get personal.** Be respectful, listen, and don't attack others or make disparaging remarks. State your point of view as unemotionally as possible.

■ **Stay until the meeting ends.** It's extremely rude to rush off before a meeting has concluded, even if you have nothing more to say. If there's a truly valid reason for you to leave at a certain time, tell the chairperson in advance and leave as unobtrusively as possible.

■ **Follow through on your commitments.** If you agree to take on any responsibility, keep your word and do a good job. Reliability and integrity should always be your goals.

Etiquette for Common Spaces

The office kitchen and/or break room, the copy room and, in some cases, the supply cabinet, belong to everybody. This means there are multiple opportunities for messing things up and irritating others. If just one person dumps a dirty plate in the kitchen sink or makes a jumble of the envelopes in the supply cabinet, everybody can be negatively affected. And if several people do these things, you've got chaos!

That's why it's important for everyone to do their fair share to keep things clean and organized. So make it a point to do the following:

- *Wash your own cups, dishes, or silverware and put them away.* Don't leave them in the sink, even if there's a cleaning service at the end of the day.

- *Make another pot of coffee if you take the last cup.* You'd be glad if someone did this for you. Model what you'd like to see.

- *Wipe out the microwave after you use it.* Food splatters while cooking more often than you might realize. Check out what you've left behind.

- *Wipe off the kitchen counter after you use it.* Crumbs or liquid on the counter can make the whole kitchen look messy.

- *Don't take food that doesn't belong to you.* This includes food that's sitting out and food in the refrigerator.

- *Throw out your leftovers.* If you stow your lunch leftovers in the office refrigerator, eat them or throw them out within a day or two. Don't let them go bad!

- *Be careful about what you cook in the microwave.* Pungent foods like broccoli, fish, and cabbage can smell up an entire office. Leave them at home.

- **Respect the trash and recycle containers.** Sort before you throw!

- **Take only what you need from the supply cabinet.** Don't hoard; leave things neat.

- **Refill the copy machine if you use the last piece of paper or if the paper supply is running low.** Give the next person a break!

- **Set the copy machine back to default if you've changed the features.** If you've ever made a bunch of copies on "landscape" when you wanted "portrait," you know how annoying it can be. Leave the machine in default status.

It may sound like a lot of rules, but etiquette for common spaces can be easily summed up: Just clean up after yourself, and leave things the way you would like to find them. Others will appreciate your thoughtfulness.

Business Etiquette Around the World

It's important to note that the customs, norms, and "rules" of etiquette discussed in this book apply specifically to the U.S. and Canadian business world. And while it's true that some of those rules also apply worldwide (e.g., arrive on time, dress appropriately, identify yourself when you place a call), others don't. So even if your conduct is considered above reproach by U.S. and Canadian standards, on foreign soil you may find yourself stepping on toes. Here are just a few examples:

- In Japan, when someone presents you with a business card, you must receive it with both hands and read it carefully. Accepting it with one hand seems cavalier, and immediately putting it in your pocket shows a lack of interest. But the worst faux pas is writing on another person's business card, which is considered extremely disrespectful.

- In the U.K., it's impolite to retain eye contact during a conversation. Look away often.

- In Japan and India, saying "no" during a discussion is considered rude, even if you disagree. The word "yes" is used often, if only to let the other party know that their meaning is understood.

- In Germany, humor is not appreciated during business meetings. So no joking around or funny stories!

- In New Zealand, business is discussed over lunch, but never over dinner. And in China, business is never discussed over any meal.

- In Egypt, it's best if you refrain from crossing your legs. Showing the sole of your foot to another person is one of their biggest insults.

When doing business internationally, especially when you are a guest in a foreign country, it's crucial to bone up on their customs and expectations to avoid making unwitting mistakes. You want to build bridges, not burn them, so be sure to do some research before you travel.

Practice kindness

I had the privilege of knowing, working with, and eventually becoming friends with Letitia Baldrige, Jacqueline Kennedy's White House chief of staff and author of numerous books on etiquette, including an excellent one entitled *Letitia Baldrige's New Complete Guide to Executive Manners*. On more than one occasion, she told me, "Sure, it's important to know how to address a visiting senior executive properly or who to introduce first in a meeting. But when in doubt, just practice kindness." And I can tell you that "Tish," as she was called, was one of the kindest people I ever knew. She had a way of making everyone feel appreciated and valued, simply by the way she treated people.

Workplace etiquette (and, for that matter, etiquette in general) is all about being kind to others. It's about understanding how your actions affect others, and then doing the kindest, most respectful thing you can think of. It's taking time to be human, to recognize others, to say "please" and "thank you," and to ensure that you're not imposing on others. That's it. Just be kind to others. You'll automatically make the world a better place.

CHAPTER 7
FIND BALANCE WITH ASSERTIVE COMMUNICATION

Have you ever had a boss who gave you an assignment, and even though you followed his orders to the letter, he berated you for doing the wrong thing? Have you ever had a co-worker agree to help you on a project, only to discover that she resented you for getting her involved and bad-mouthed you behind your back? How about the annoying experience of giving explicit instructions to a temp, and coming back from vacation to find half of the tasks left undone?

All of these are instances of communication gone awry. In the examples above, the boss was obviously unclear about what he expected. The co-worker may not have understood what was being asked of her, or she may have simply been too passive to say "no." And the temp may have been daydreaming rather that listening or possibly agreeing to do those tasks, then saying "no" indirectly by doing an incomplete job. Whatever the reason, the original message was somehow ignored, garbled, or misinterpreted.

Communication mishaps are the driving force behind a huge percentage of on-the-job errors, hard feelings among employees, and poor job performance on every level. Miscommunication costs companies millions of dollars, results in job loss and stymied career growth, makes simple tasks ridiculously complex, and eats away at otherwise good relationships. For these reasons and more, it's absolutely essential that you learn to communicate as clearly and accurately as you can in the workplace, no matter who you're dealing with.

Four Styles of Communication

Like everyone else, you've been communicating since the day you were born. You began by screeching loudly to tell those around you that you wanted or needed something. Then, over the years, you slowly adopted more sophisticated and refined ways of getting your message across. (I hope!) By now, you've developed your own unique communication style—or set of styles, as you communicate differently depending on where you are, who you're with, and what you're doing. (For instance, I obviously communicated very differently with my somewhat formal grandmother than I did with my best girlfriends.) One style will most likely predominate, but is it the one that will work best for you professionally and personally?

From what I've observed, most people aren't even aware that they have a communication style, much less what it is and how to tweak it for maximum success. So let's begin by taking a look at the four main styles of communication—passive, aggressive, passive-aggressive, and assertive—and then discovering which one matches yours most closely.

1. *Passive (the doormat)*

The passive person is overly submissive, eager to avoid conflict, and often shy. She wants so much to be "nice" that she often agrees to do things she doesn't want to do. Women often fall into this trap because they were raised to be compliant, sweet, easygoing, and "good." Saying "no," standing up for their rights, or doing anything other than what is demanded of them goes against what they were taught. They automatically submerge their own needs and desires in favor of being seen as likable and cooperative.

A passive person says things like, "Whatever the group decides is all right with me" or, "I go along to get along."

The unspoken message she sends is, "My thoughts and feelings are not as important as other people's." As a result, she is often disregarded and disrespected by others.

2. *Aggressive (the steamroller)*

The aggressive person gets his way by bullying others into doing what he wants. He yells, complains, attacks others verbally, and doesn't care about other people's rights and feelings as long as he gets his own way. He can be superior, self-righteous, intimidating, and insulting and has learned that he can browbeat others into submission.

An aggressive person may say things like, "That's the stupidest thing I've ever heard!" or, "You're 100 percent *wrong!*"

The unspoken message he sends is, "My thoughts and feelings are more important than everyone else's." Because of this, he is often resented, disliked, and opposed by others.

3. *Passive-aggressive (the doormat with spikes)*

The passive-aggressive person pretends to go along with others and agrees with things he doesn't really agree with. He has a hard time directly refusing the requests of others, so he says "no" indirectly through his actions by procrastinating, forgetting to do what he promised, losing things, and so on.

A passive-aggressive person may say things like, "Sure, I'd be happy to do that for you," but he never gets around to doing it.

The unspoken message he sends is, "I seem to be a polite, friendly, cooperative person, but I'm actually very manipulative. Don't count on me." As a result, others are often uneasy around him, and a lack of trust eats away at his relationships.

4. *Assertive (the pillar)*

The assertive person expresses her needs clearly and respectfully and stands up for her own beliefs and rights while respecting the beliefs and rights of others. This means she considers her own needs *and* the needs of others and is open to compromise. She uses facts, rather than judgments, to make her points and tries never to exaggerate. She also uses "I" statements as much as possible, telling others how she feels and what she thinks, rather than accusing them.

An assertive person says things like, "I believe that I'm being overlooked," instead of, "You're overlooking me." Or, "I'm angry with you," instead of "You make me angry." (She also feels comfortable expressing her positive emotions, like, "I really enjoy being with you," or "I cherish our friendship.")

The unspoken message she sends is, "My thoughts and feelings and your thoughts and feelings are equally important. Let's discuss our problems rationally and respectfully." Because of this, she is respected and trusted by others and seen as a team player with high confidence and self-esteem.

What's Your Communication Style?

To find your typical style of communication, choose the response that sounds most like you:

1. **When you're offering a solution to a problem at a department meeting, a co-worker cuts you off before you can finish.**

    a. You stare at the other person and continue talking louder and faster.

    b. You stop talking, sit back in your chair, and allow the other person to take over.

    c. You lean into the conversation and give a "one minute" hand signal to the other person. Once you've finished, you ask for that person's input.

    d. You stop talking, glare at the other person, and pout through the rest of the meeting.

2. **Your supervisor gives you a verbal okay to take Friday off, then tells you Thursday night that the workload is unusually high, so you'll be needed on Friday.**

    a. You say angrily, "I have a problem with that. You told me I could have the time off. How come you never do this to any of the night crew? Why do I get punished just because I work days?"

    b. You say, "But I thought you said you didn't need me." Then you sigh and say, "Okay, I'll be here."

    c. You say, "It sounds like this is important. You know I'm committed to making this department run well, but I made important plans for tomorrow. Perhaps there's another solution, like working late tonight or coming in over the weekend."

    d. You grudgingly agree, "All right, I'll come in." Then you call in sick.

3. **During a meeting, one of your co-workers takes credit for an idea you came up with.**

    a. In front of everyone, you shout, "Hey, you just stole my idea! I'm not going to sit here and let you pretend you dreamed it up yourself!"

    b. You say nothing during or after the meeting and spend the next several days depressed, berating yourself for being stupid and getting taken advantage of.

    c. You confront her by saying, "When you act like my ideas are your own, I feel like I can't trust you. I shared my ideas with you in confidence, and you broke that trust."

    d. You tell everyone behind her back that she stole your idea.

4. **To increase your ability to serve customers more efficiently, you were promised a larger office. But when it's time to move in, you are told, "Sorry, it didn't work out the way we thought," and you're given a smaller office than before.**

a. You storm into your boss's office to complain and accuse him of lying to you.

b. You shake your head and think, "Well, isn't this just my luck!"

c. You go to your boss, acknowledge that things don't always work out as planned, but tell him that in order to best serve your customers, you will need more space. You offer alternatives and stay open to creative solutions.

d. You shut yourself in your new office and refuse to talk to anyone for the next week.

5. **You're asked to take over the job of ordering supplies for the entire department. But your plate is already so full that you have been working overtime on your own just to keep up.**

a. You tell your boss that you can't possibly handle this huge chore and if pressed, you'll have to quit your job without notice.

b. You say, "Okay, but I've got an awful lot to do, and now I'm not sure everything will get done."

c. You explain to your boss you're already working off the clock to handle your current responsibilities. Maintaining a high standard of quality may not be possible if you take on another chore. You suggest a round-robin style of supply ordering instead.

    d. You say nothing, roll your eyes, and throw the ordering materials into your inbox. Then you order supplies only sporadically. If anyone complains, you say, "Would *you* like to do it? Be my guest!"

If you chose mostly A's, you have an *aggressive* style of communication. You tend to lash out at others, push their buttons, and trample on their feelings. In general, you'll want to dial it down and think more about the rights and feelings of others.

If you chose mostly B's, you have a *passive* style of communication. You let others walk all over you and rarely voice your opinions. Do your best to say "no" more often, and realize that your thoughts, feelings, and rights are just as important as anyone else's.

If you chose mostly C's, you have an *assertive* style of communication. You stand up for your own rights and the rights of others. You're fair, you listen to others, and you're good at compromising. Keep up the good work!

If you chose mostly D's, you have a *passive-aggressive* style of communication. You often say "yes" when you mean "no." Then you find ways of saying "no" indirectly, like procrastinating or forgetting. You hide your anger until it bubbles over, surprising others with its intensity. Usually, they have no idea that you've been stuffing down your negative emotions. Instead, speak up for yourself and express your feelings directly and honestly.

For each of your responses, ask yourself the following questions:

- What's the true driving motive behind my response?
- What will the result of my response be?
- What do I stand to gain or lose by this response?
- What skills do I need to acquire in order to change any passive, aggressive, or passive-aggressive responses to assertive ones?

Becoming More Assertive

Assertiveness—standing up for your rights and expressing yourself clearly, while respecting the rights of others—maximizes your chances of communicating successfully. If positivity and passion are the states of being most necessary for achieving success in life, then assertiveness is the most important tool. When you're assertive, you're much more likely to get your message across with clarity, solve problems successfully, facilitate teamwork, and preserve and promote good relationships. Others will understand where you're coming from, how you feel, and what you want, yet they will feel respected, listened to, and a part of the team. Both parties will be making decisions and solving problems together. It's quite simply the best way to communicate that's ever been devised.

However, being assertive isn't automatic. It takes some thought, some skill building, and a lot of practice. Although I've taught assertiveness for the past 30 years and think of myself as very assertive, here's a very recent example of a time I did not communicate assertively and immediately regretted it. I spend four to six weeks a year working in a smallish town in the Midwest, and one day, I happened to be talking to a local minister there who asked me if I had found a church yet, hinting that he'd like me to come to his services. Caught off guard, I replied, "Well, I'm not around here very much so I wasn't thinking of joining a church … " as my voice trailed off into a feeble murmur. I should have known better. It was a completely passive reply, and not at all truthful! In fact, I'm not a churchgoer at all. What I should have said was, "Thanks so much for asking, but I'm not a churchgoer," which would have been direct, honest, *inarguable*, and assertive. But I fell into the trap of being passive as a way of being polite. He immediately replied, "Well, it doesn't matter to us if you're not around much. We can sign you up anyway! Just come whenever you're here." I was trapped by my own lack of assertiveness and forced into back-pedaling on my original false excuse. I guess this incident shows there's always room for improvement!

When you're first turned on to the idea of becoming more asser-tive, it's tempting to think, "Good! Now I'll be able to go back and tell my nasty ex-landlord what I've always thought of him … " But remember, much as I might empathize with your motives, that's not what real assertiveness is all about—it's never about pouncing on someone and telling him off. It's about thoughtful, measured, *balanced* communication, born out of respect for both yourself and all others, and evidenced by everything that you say and do (even if you *do* have a nasty ex-landlord who's standing right in front of you in the grocery store checkout line!).

Besides being the best way to communicate clearly and solve problems effectively, being assertive is also about expressing your *positive* feelings, which can be very freeing and joy-producing! When you're truly assertive, you feel quietly, positively powerful— you become certain that you can handle whatever comes along. Because you say what you mean, you're allowed to say "yes" as well as "no"; express your love for others; compliment others without restraint; be comfortable with virtually anyone; and confidently make decisions about your life, your career, and your relationships. When you're assertive, you can truly be yourself and feel good about it. Take it from me: It's a great way to live your life.

Nine steps to communicating more assertively

If you're like most people, you aren't naturally assertive. Most of us were brought up in ways that steered us toward some other style. So learning to communicate assertively will be a process for you, one that requires you to examine your own behavior and really think about what you're doing and saying.

You can begin by doing your best to incorporate the following whenever you communicate:

1. **Use "I" statements.** When you tell others where you stand, strive to put your feelings and thoughts into an "I" format, rather than a "you" format. Instead of saying, "*You* leave me in the lurch with your last-minute cancellations," say, "*I* feel I can't rely on you when you cancel at the last minute." Rather than saying, "*You* frustrate me," say, "*I* feel frustrated." This way, you can express yourself without accusing the other person. You can take responsibility for your own feelings, rather than blaming someone else. You focus on the problem at hand, and your listener is less likely to become defensive and shut down, because he doesn't feel accused.

2. **Keep your responses brief.** Don't keep talking once you've made your point. Too much talking doesn't make your case stronger; it does just the opposite by obscuring your message and tiring or annoying your listener. As a result, your message can get lost in the shuffle.

3. **Slow down your rate of speech.** Although nervousness can spur you to talk quickly, rapid speech can be hard to follow and make you seem uneasy or lacking in self-confidence. By

slowing your speech, you'll appear more self-assured, your message will be clearer and easier to decipher, and there will be less of a chance that you'll say something you hadn't intended.

4. **Deepen your voice.** Whenever possible, speak in a lower register (while still sounding natural) to convey authority and self-assurance. Higher-pitched voices can be associated with immaturity. Women, in particular, should stay away from that extra-high pitch pattern used for greeting long-lost friends and talking to babies—the antithesis of assertive communication! Keep your pitch low but within your normal range.

5. **Watch your nonverbal messages.** Be sure your face and body are sending messages that are congruent with your words. (Telling your listener that you're very excited while you're slumping in your chair doesn't work well.)

6. **Truly listen.** Listening closely to the person you're communicating with is one of the basic tenets of assertive communication. Give that person your full attention, listen more than you speak, stay engaged while listening, ask clarifying (but not nosy) questions, and smile, when appropriate. Most important of all, look for points of commonality in what's being said—what can you both agree on? What do you both want? These will be your starting points for building rapport, and, if necessary, finding compromise.

7. **Maintain eye contact.** By now you know about the importance of eye contact. Look the other person directly in the eye, but break eye contact just briefly after several seconds to avoid seeming hostile or aggressive. Then resume it.

8. **Control your emotions.** Don't allow your emotions to control what you do or say. Expressing how you feel is a good thing, but letting your feelings run away with you is not. This

means getting furious, yelling, whining, crying, and feeling sorry for yourself have no place in assertive communication. Explain what's on your mind, but keep your emotions from taking over. (However, we're going to talk about crying again later, in chapter 9. It sometimes happens beyond our control, and there's an assertive way to handle it, either for yourself or for others.)

9. **Say "no" when appropriate.** Most of us don't say "no" often enough because it's uncomfortable. But the next time someone asks you to do something that you truly feel is an imposition, politely refuse, knowing that you have every right to do so. You might say, "No, I can't do that right now" or, "No, there's just too much on my plate." Then, if you must explain further, keep it short. Saying "no" may be awkward or difficult, but it's an important part of standing up for yourself, and it definitely becomes easier over time. And you might be surprised when the other person not only accepts what you've said, but respects you for it!

Being Assertive Means ...

- You are accountable for your own behavior
- You decide for yourself what you will and will not do, and you feel free to change your mind when necessary
- You are responsible for solving your *own* problems, but not other people's problems (although you always assist others whenever possible)
- You express yourself honestly, directly, and considerately

■ With every action, word, and deed, you respect and protect your rights *and* the rights of those around you

The difference between assertiveness and aggressiveness

At first glance, being assertive and being aggressive may seem an awful lot alike. They both involve standing up for your rights, saying what's on your mind, and getting your message across clearly. But they are very different. The main difference between the two is that assertiveness aims at achieving *balance*, while aggressiveness aims at *winning*. Assertiveness is about working *with* people; aggressiveness is about working *against* them. Here are a few definitions:

■ **You're being assertive if ...**

You are forthright about your wants and needs, but you always consider the rights, feelings, and desires of others. You ask for what you want, knowing full well that you may or may not get it. Your goal is to find solutions, rather than to win. Being more assertive helps you express your feelings more effectively, communicate more clearly, gain the respect of others, and work with others to find common ground and solve problems. Over time, assertiveness can improve your productivity on the job, self-esteem, personal relationships, and satisfaction in life.

■ **You're being aggressive if ...**

You do what's best for you *without* regard for the rights, feelings, or desires of others. You take what you want and don't ask permission. Your goals are to control the situation (or the people involved) and win. Over time, being aggressive can destroy your relationships with others by impairing communication, increasing ill feelings toward you, decreasing cooperation, and making people want to work against you.

Should You *Always* Be Assertive?

Assertiveness is the best way to communicate in any kind of relationship because of its clarity, respectfulness, and ability to clear the air. But there are times when being assertive just might get you into trouble, and in those cases, being passive could be a better alternative.

For example, let's say someone cuts in front of you when you're waiting in line to buy movie tickets. Your assertive (and completely reasonable) response to that person might be, "Excuse me. I'm in line here. The line forms back there, behind those people." However, let's change this scenario just one tiny bit: Let's say the person who jumped in ahead of you happens to be 6'6", seems to be in a bad mood, and smells like whiskey. In that case, it might be a heck of a lot smarter if you said nothing! Passive behavior might also be your choice when you want to defer to someone else's seniority or expertise, when the situation or issue is not a priority, or when you're just trying to keep a low profile.

But how about when you're interacting with a person who has a history of treating you with disrespect or the stakes are so high that you really need to be heard and understood? In cases like these, instead of becoming aggressive, I suggest using a technique called "escalating assertion." Let's say the office bully is angry with you and just called you a very nasty name in front of 10 other people. You take him aside, adopt a firm stance, and do the following:

1. Sum up what happened. ("You insulted me in front of others.")

2. Express how it affected you. ("I was angry and embarrassed.")

3. State your needs. ("If you have something to say to me, I want you to say it in private.")

4. Relate the consequences. ("If you let me know what's on your mind before it gets to the point of name-calling, we'll be able to solve the problem more calmly and efficiently.")

This very useful technique allows you to express yourself without ever becoming aggressive. While being passive may sometimes be a necessary choice, I recommend against aggressiveness and passive-aggressiveness *in all situations.* Both always do more harm than good, and once you've mastered the assertive style of communication, they should be completely unnecessary. Plus, you never want to model a behavior that you, yourself, would not want directed toward you—this is another version of the "do unto others" rule!

Using Assertiveness to Solve Problems

Assertiveness is a balancing act. You want to be:

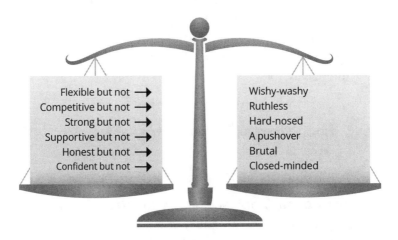

Flexible but not →	Wishy-washy
Competitive but not →	Ruthless
Strong but not →	Hard-nosed
Supportive but not →	A pushover
Honest but not →	Brutal
Confident but not →	Closed-minded

It may take a while for you to get used to communicating this way. Be aware that you'll need to put some time and thought into what you want to say *before* it comes out of your mouth. Otherwise, you'll just fall back into old communication styles. So before you jump up and start expressing yourself, take a moment to define the problem, decide what you want to say, and come up with a specific request.

Define the problem

Here's the scenario:

> You're working hard on a project with a rapidly approaching deadline when your boss suddenly hands you a second project and asks that it be done ASAP. You feel frustrated, angry, and upset by how little regard he has for you in your current situation. How are you supposed to do two things at once? You realize that you need to stand up for yourself and rectify the situation.

Before you say anything, you need to:

- **Become clear about your goals.** What exactly do you want from this exchange with your boss? Typical goals might include solving a problem, establishing your position, clarifying instructions, and finding common ground, just to name a few. In this case, let's say you come up with three goals:

  1. Clarify which project takes priority

  2. Find out how long you currently have to complete each one

  3. Adjust the time frame for completion, if necessary

- **Think through the facts of the situation.** Forget about your anger, frustration, and hurt feelings; they will just get in the way of thinking clearly and delivering a coherent message. Instead, focus on the facts, which are:

  1. You were given two projects with conflicting deadlines

  2. There's no way you'll be able to complete both in a timely manner

Carefully decide what to say and how to say it

Think through what you want to say and how to say it before you approach your boss. Remember these four important points:

- **Make a statement.** Begin by laying out the facts of the situation. You might say, "I now have two projects that need to be done ASAP, and I'm already in a time crunch on the first one." Be direct without being accusatory. Don't fall into the passive mode and turn the statement into a question, as in, "Don't you think it's too much to expect me to do two high-priority projects at once?" Instead, explain unemotionally that you're in an impossible situation.

- **Limit the details.** Just relate the details necessary to explain the problem and eliminate the misunderstanding.

- **Look your listener in the eye, and be aware of your body language.** Make eye contact. Resist the urge to cross your arms, clasp your hands, or hunch your shoulders, which can make it look like you're unwilling to communicate. Sit or stand with your arms relaxed by your side to show that you're open and approachable.

- **Use a cooperative, non-adversarial tone of voice.** Avoid using an aggressive, loud, or forceful tone of voice. Your aim is to come to an agreement, not bowl the listener over. At the same time, don't be apologetic, timid, or whiny. You have every right to stand up for your rights, and your voice should reflect that.

Make a specific request

Once you've explained the situation, ask for something well defined and reasonable. In this case, you might ask your boss for more time to complete each project. In any case, you should:

- **Be specific.** Avoid generalities or murky language, like asking for the listener to "take a more active role" or "be more flexible."

- **Limit your requests to one or two.** Don't ask for too much at once. If you come in with a laundry list of requests, you'll probably be turned down.

- **Keep it positive.** Tell the listener what you *do* want, not what you *don't* want.

- **Focus on behavior.** You can ask the listener to change something he *does*, but don't ask him to change the way he *thinks* or *feels* (which is a much more difficult proposition).

When you're ready, find an appropriate time and place to have a chat with the person in question. Don't accost him when he's with others or march into his office and demand to be heard. Try to catch him when he's alone, ask if he's got a minute, close the door behind you (if you can), and speak to him respectfully.

Speaking Habits That Diminish Your Power

You may be speaking in a perfectly assertive tone of voice; you may look confident and professional; your message may be absolutely justifiable. But if you fall into certain power-sapping speaking habits, you can appear weak, indecisive, and unconvincing, which can undermine your cause. Avoid the following, especially when you want to appear powerful:

- **Verbal crutches:** Peppering your speech with filler words like "um," "uh," "okay," and "you know" interferes with the clarity of your message and makes you look uncertain and unprepared. Teach yourself to be silent while thinking on your feet. You don't have to fill every inch of air space when you're talking. A measured pause can make you appear more thoughtful, intelligent, and confident.

- **Qualifiers:** Disclaimers used at the beginning of a sentence, like "I might not know," or "You would know better than I," or "Correct me if I'm wrong ... " imply that you don't know what you're talking about. You might find yourself using qualifiers to protect yourself in case you happen to be wrong, but they will just make you look weak. Get right down to it and make your statement.

- **Tag questions:** When you make a statement, then immediately add a question like, "Don't you think?" or "Am I right?" or "Does that make sense?" you're asking the listener for validation. This implies that you are unsure about your message and/or yourself. Leave off the tag question.

- **Excluders:** Excluders are statements that disrupt rapport because they assume something about the listener that may not be true. Examples include: "How was your Christmas holiday?" (Problem: Not everyone celebrates Christmas.) Or, "When you were in college ... " (Problem: Not everyone went to college.) Or, "Did you and your wife ... ?" (Problem: Not everyone has a wife). These kinds of statements are not only alienating, but they can put the listener in the awkward position of having to reveal something about himself that he hadn't intended, such as, "Oh, I didn't go to college" or "I'm not actually married." Try your best not to make statements that may exclude your listeners. Of course, racist, sexist, ageist, and politically charged statements are also excluders—not to mention the fact that they're aggressive, inappropriate, and just plain indefensible.

Listening and asking questions

All right, let's say you've laid out your case to your boss and made your request. Now it's time to stop talking and just listen! Utilize all of your active listening skills. Give him your full attention, look for feedback and clues in his body language, make every effort to understand his point of view, and try not to think about what you're going to say next, as it will keep you from listening fully. Let him continue, uninterrupted, until he's completely finished.

Then ask questions that will help clarify his position. His answers will let you know if your message got through. And you'll find out more about how he thinks and who he is.

Asking the Right Questions at the Right Time

Asking questions is one of the best ways find out what another person is thinking and/or feeling. There are five major types of questions:

- **Open-ended questions:** These questions, which can't be answered with a simple "yes" or "no," allow the listener to talk. If you want a person to reveal himself or expand on a topic, ask him an open-ended question, as in, "What changes would you like to see in our business?" or "How do you feel about the managerial candidates?" Open-ended questions are good for building rapport because they encourage revelations and openness. The downside is they can invite digression and overtalking.

- **Closed questions:** Typically answered with a "yes," a "no," or some other short, specific reply, closed questions are the favorite of trial lawyers. An example of a closed question is, "Were you aware that $1 million was deposited into your bank account on February

12?" Closed questions are used to guide or limit a discussion or discover or confirm facts. However, since they limit discussion, they aren't good for building rapport.

- **Probing questions:** These go right to the heart of the matter and are used to get specific information or gain insight into another's opinions or point of view. Examples are, "What would it take to get you to agree to this proposal?" or "Why exactly are you interested in changing your cable company?"

- **Confirming questions:** Salespeople often use confirming questions to find out if a customer really got their message. For example, they might say, "Which features on this smartphone do you think will help you out the most?" If the customer has no answer, they know it's time to go back to the drawing board.

- **Summary confirmation questions:** The purpose of summary confirmation questions is to sum up the message you've received from another and check that you understood her correctly. For example, you might say, "So you would like me to come up with an ad campaign for Coke® that's colorful, energetic, fun, and sexy, but doesn't alienate older people." (Notice that this "question" is actually worded as a *statement* and is intended to elicit agreement.)

Learning to ask the right questions at the right time can bring you a treasure trove of information. Maybe it's because of my background as a psychologist, but I really like to ask open-ended questions and sit back and hear what the other person has to say. People can be so interesting!

But if you want to get a conversation started, keep it going, and help it stay on course, I find it's best to use a mix of open and closed questions. Probing questions can be added when you need specific information, and confirming or summary confirmation questions will help you find out if your message got across while you're wrapping things up.

Reaching an understanding

Let's say that you and your boss have now finished your discussion, and hopefully, you're about to come to some sort of consensus. Because assertive communication is all about achieving balance, you won't necessarily get everything you've requested. For example, he might say, "All right, let's postpone the deadline for completing that first project for a day or two. But I need you to complete the second project right away." Or he might say, "I need both projects to stay on track, so work overtime as long as it takes to meet both deadlines." But no matter what happens, you will have expressed yourself clearly and respectfully and shown that you are professional, conscientious and, ultimately, a team player. And that's a win for you, regardless of how this incident pans out.

Communication Skills—the Key to Success

No matter what kind of business you're involved in or what your position, you're going to spend a lot of time communicating with others—receiving and giving instructions; making phone calls; explaining yourself; asking for things; dealing with clients, co-workers, bosses, and assistants; selling yourself; representing your company; and participating in meetings. In all of these endeavors, your key to success will lie in your ability to convey your thoughts, feelings, objectives, and intentions clearly and accurately in ways that others can understand and accept—in short, your success lies in your ability to communicate assertively.

Becoming more assertive will pave the way to achieving both your personal and professional goals. By standing up for your rights in an appropriate and effective manner, you'll improve your problem-solving ability, establish better relationships, earn the respect and cooperation of others, and open doors to new career opportunities. You'll also gain a greater understanding of yourself and belief in your own value, which will increase your self-confidence. And you'll find it just gets easier and easier to get to win-win, which, after all, is the number one goal of assertive communication.

CHAPTER 8

GAIN POWER WITHOUT SACRIFICING INTEGRITY

Ask almost any powerful, influential person—Bill Gates, Hillary Clinton, Warren Buffet, Oprah Winfrey, or a similar bigwig—and that person will tell you he or she was once like you, trying to get a foot in the door, wondering how to make a stellar impression, and determined to get ahead. Everybody has to start somewhere! You, however, are further down the road than most, because you already know plenty of secrets to success. You know how to walk, talk, and look like a winner. You know that it's absolutely crucial to infuse everything you do with positivity and passion. You've learned the rules of office etiquette and discovered how to fit in at work without getting lost in the crowd. You understand how to stand up for your rights and work effectively with others by communicating assertively.

Your next big task will be to demonstrate to one and all that you're destined for the major leagues! That's right; you must convince others that you're a born leader and that you're ready to sit at the table—even if there's no room at the moment. A good way to start is by modeling the behavior of the well-established, noteworthy people who are all around you.

10 Critical Skills You Need to Become Powerful and Influential

I've known scores of important, eminent people, and in every case, it appears that their rise to the top was no accident. All of them— and I mean *all*—have certain qualities that make them worthy and effective as leaders. Because of these qualities, they are able to draw clients, sell products, form solid bonds with useful people and organizations, smooth the ruffled feathers of those who might otherwise have quashed a deal, and inspire others to follow them. With this in mind, I've come up with a list of characteristics that you'll need to cultivate in order to take your career to the next level:

1. *The ability to work with people:* Powerful people understand that they need to get along with others to get the job done, to network effectively, and to build and maintain their careers. If people don't like you or don't agree with the way you work, they'll balk at your ideas and find ways to avoid working with you. As a result, you'll end up spending the bulk of your time arguing with people, getting frustrated, and spinning your wheels. It's vital that you attract and maintain as much support as possible. Nobody climbs to the top or stays there without the help of others.

2. *Self-assurance, confidence, and social poise:* If you want others to believe in you, your ideas, and your ability to lead, you need to believe in yourself first. Those who are unsure of themselves, professionally and/or personally, will be mistrusted by others and have a hard time getting people to get on board. Developing a healthy level of self-confidence— without ever crossing over to smugness or cockiness—is essential to your success.

3. *Consideration for others:* It's no secret that people work harder when they feel valued, appreciated, and heard. A

leader who considers the feelings of others, recognizes their accomplishments, and appreciates a job well done is much more likely to keep employees engaged and motivated than one who is neglectful, punitive, or rude. Be polite and appreciative; it will come back to you!

4. *Tact and diplomacy:* Powerful, influential people know how to speak to others in ways that are understood and accepted. Realizing that a defensive listener is much harder (if not impossible) to persuade, they ruffle others' feathers as little as possible and work toward collaborative agreement whenever practicable.

5. *Self-control:* The first rule of power and influence is that both must always be tempered with discipline and objectivity. If you allow your ego or emotions to dictate your actions, you can doom relationships, projects, or even an entire business (along with your career!). Learn to be ruled by your head, rather than your feelings.

6. *The ability to analyze facts and solve problems:* Getting to the heart of the problem and finding effective solutions are two vitally important skills for any leader. Focusing on the facts, ignoring distractions, and seeing things for what they are (rather than what they seem to be) are crucial skills when seeking win-win solutions.

7. *Decisiveness:* Powerful people act; they make decisions and they go with them. Their decisions may not always be right, but once the wheels are in motion, *something* gets done. (They also understand that a change in direction is always possible once things get rolling, especially if new factors become part of the mix.) After gathering as much information as possible, you'll need to bite the bullet and make a choice.

8. **High standards:** A company's ethics, ideals, and culture begin at the top with the leader, then trickle down through the ranks. As a leader, you must set the bar high for yourself and others and model conduct that is above reproach. If you slack off in any way, others will surely follow suit.

9. **The ability to prioritize and organize effectively:** Powerful people often need to do a lot in a short amount of time. As a leader, you must become an expert at prioritizing, planning, and executing tasks with a maximum of efficiency. Make to-do lists in order of importance and follow them. Tune out distractions. Don't waste time on things that don't really matter.

10. **The ability to delegate:** A powerful, influential person functions much like the conductor of an orchestra: He surrounds himself with great musicians, decides what they will play, then waves a baton and lets them do their thing. He doesn't try to play the instruments, because he knows it isn't going to work. Instead, he trusts those around him to do their jobs effectively and on time. You do the same.

Even if you're not in management yet, start incorporating these skills and characteristics in your work and personal lives *today*. The more often you practice them, the more second nature they will become, and eventually, they will become your habits. Be excellent and act like a leader every day!

The Importance of a Having a Mentor

A mentor is an adviser, somebody who takes a personal interest in helping you learn, progress, and thrive. He or she is wiser and more experienced than you and has special knowledge about your field, business in general, and the ways of the world. A mentor might be one of your teachers, coaches, parents, family friends, fellow employees, or even your boss. There are also mentoring programs at many colleges and universities, in which professionals from the local community work with interested students. (I was a Big Sister in the Big Brothers Big Sisters of the Bay Area organization when I lived in Oakland, California, and I currently serve as a mentor for business, education, and psychology students at Cal Poly University in San Luis Obispo, California.) Just about everyone who becomes powerful and influential has had several mentors, and often one in particular has made a very positive impact on their careers.

One of my own wonderful mentors was Doris Ross, program director of Crestwood Hospital in Sacramento back in the 1980s when I served as an intern there. Doris took a liking to me, and when my internship was completed, she hired me as a psychiatric aide. Then she almost immediately promoted me to psychiatric assistant. One of my responsibilities in this new job was to give in-services (training programs for the staff), which I really enjoyed. And evidently Doris thought I was good at it, because she soon championed me for the job of in-house trainer for the entire hospital.

Doris walked me straight into the hospital administrator's office and told him flat-out, "Denise is good with patients and staff, and she's also a great speaker. I think you should make her our in-house trainer. What's more, I think you should pay her $1,500 a month." Believe it or not, that was very good money back then, and literally more than

I ever thought I would make. I was shocked when I heard Doris suggest that amount and even more shocked when the administrator agreed without hesitation. The upshot was that not only did Doris negotiate a great salary for me, but she set me on a path that culminated in my becoming clinical director of the entire corporation a few years later. Now that's a great mentor. Thanks, Doris!

Besides meeting with you regularly to give advice and listen to your questions and problems, a mentor may also provide valuable networking opportunities, write letters of recommendation, tell you about job opportunities, and steer you in the right direction when you're going off course. A good mentor can be enormously important to you and your career, but how do you find one? Here are a few ideas:

- **Get into a mentoring program.** Some companies have their own mentoring programs. If you're lucky enough to work in a place like this, your HR department can give you the details.

- **Search your mental address book.** Ask yourself if there's already a "mentor-in-waiting" in your life—someone whose knowledge and expertise you haven't tapped yet. It's possible that person is just waiting for you to ask!

- **Look in your own backyard.** Look for people in your workplace who enjoy helping others succeed—especially people younger than themselves. These individuals are natural-born mentors who may already be guiding some of your peers and might be happy to take you on as well—providing you are worthy of mentoring.

■ ***Be a standout employee.*** Apply the principles discussed in chapter 5, "How to Fit In and Present a Winning Image." Someone may notice you and be impressed. Be ready with a question or well-thought-out comment that can break the ice when you have a chance to chat with a would-be mentor.

Remember, mentors *want* to mentor—it's their natural state of being. But no one wants to mentor someone who is negative, unmotivated, unproductive, or just plain unpleasant to be around. Be the kind of person *you'd* like to mentor someday!

How to Treat Your Boss

I've been a boss for a long time, but I've also worked for plenty of bosses throughout my career. And I know that of all the relationships you develop at work, by far the most important is the one you have with your boss. During the time you work together, that person will decide what you do, how much power you're given, if and when you'll be promoted, and even whether or not you'll keep your job. So, obviously, you'll need to guard this relationship with everything you've got, and take extra special care in all your dealings with her. Here are four important rules to keep in mind:

■ ***Make your boss your first priority.*** If you're on the phone and your boss calls or comes by your office, get off the phone right away (or put the call on hold) and attend to her. Don't keep her waiting! If she wants to set a meeting for a certain time, accommodate her; reschedule your other meetings, appointments, or lunch dates, if necessary. And when she gives you an assignment, get on it right away and follow up promptly. No procrastinating! Your goal should be to make her feel she's the most important person in your life—at least in your work life—because she *is*.

- **Hear what she's really saying.** Listen carefully when your boss speaks, and don't just dwell on her words. Do your best to understand what she *means*. For example, let's say she stops by your desk for an update on a big project and, while there, reaches over and straightens up some messy papers in your inbox. Her spoken message may be: "I've come to hear about your progress on the project." But her unspoken message is: "I like things to be neat." In response to both of these messages, you should work diligently on the project *and* tidy up your desk.

- **Support her in every way you can.** Sing your boss's praises to everyone, and do so sincerely. During meetings, back her up when she presents ideas or assertions, and never disagree with her in front of others. Don't *ever* talk about her behind her back, even to your best friend, as things like this have a way of getting back to people. Do everything you can to build this relationship and avoid sabotaging it.

- **Receive criticism graciously.** Because you're not perfect, sooner or later your boss is going to offer you some "constructive feedback" (aka criticism), or at least attempt to give you a few pointers. And when she does, it's important to refrain from reacting emotionally or becoming defensive. Privately, you may think she has it all wrong. But she may be giving you vital feedback on how you appear to her and others. Consider her criticism a favor; if you can nip your shortcomings in the bud and improve your performance and professional image, you'll be ahead of the game. Receive the comments calmly and diplomatically, and ask for clarification if you need it. You'll demonstrate that you're thoughtful, conscientious, and eager to learn. And she may come away admiring you and liking you even more!

A Few Rules of Boss Etiquette

Being courteous to everyone is a given. But a few specifics pertain especially to your treatment of your boss:

- **Let her sit first.** At a meeting that you both attend, wait to see where your boss sits before choosing your own seat. Sitting in her chair is a big faux pas!

- **Don't touch her unless invited.** Patting your boss on the back, hugging her, putting your arm around her, or touching her in any other way can be seen as crossing a line. Engage in reciprocal touching only—that is, if she initiates a handshake (or a hug), you respond. Otherwise, hands off.

- **Don't touch her possessions unless invited.** Don't take objects from her desk or shelves to inspect more closely or move her things to make room for your own without asking first. This is her territory; don't invade it.

- **Don't bring food or drinks into her cubicle or office.** If she wants you to eat or drink, she'll let you know that it's a lunch meeting (or something similar). Otherwise, no chowing down or setting your coffee cup on her desk.

- **Knock before entering if her office door is closed.** You may think that since you work for her, you're welcome anytime. You aren't. Knock first.

Always remember that your relationship with your boss is the bedrock of your career and the reason for your presence in the company. If this relationship is shaky, unpleasant, or fraught with tension, it will be hard for you to grow and flourish. But if it's solid, and especially if she can see herself in you and really wants to mentor you, you can develop and expand, take on more responsibilities, become noticed by others, and grow in your career.

The Difficult Boss

I sincerely hope that your boss will be wonderfully nice, caring, clear about what he wants, and appreciative of all you do. But at some point during your career, you'll probably find yourself working for somebody who doesn't have these qualities—someone who's a difficult boss. And when you do, you'll need certain coping strategies to see you through until you can move on to a more positive situation.

Although there are all kinds of difficult bosses, here are four that seem to show up in the workplace most often. Check out the descriptions of them below, along with my suggestions for holding on to your job and your sanity if you find yourself working for one of them. (Be aware that some bosses are a combination of more than one type.)

- **The Grouch:** The Grouch is just plain negative about everything. He's a big complainer: Nothing is ever done properly, the world is against him, everything is incredibly difficult—you get the idea. You might hear him say things like, "Well, it's about time you got this report finished. I suppose it's full of mistakes … " or "Doesn't anyone actually *work* in this office? Why am I the only one who ever gets anything done around here?"

Here's my advice: Do *not* become swallowed up by his negativity and take on this attitude yourself (which may be harder than it sounds). Instead, keep a respectful distance, be succinct and well organized when interacting with him, stay positive *without* trying to change his outlook, and avoid arguing. As much as possible, let his negativity wash over you, like water over pebbles in a stream. Understand that this is who the Grouch is, but it doesn't have to affect *you* unless you let it.

- ▪ ***The Crazy Maker:*** The Crazy Maker asks you for one thing, then decides he wants something else, but doesn't tell you. Instead, he expects you to read his mind and do something quite different than originally requested. For example, he might say, "From now on, I want you to listen in on all my phone calls so you'll be up to speed on what I'm doing." Then he yells at you for listening to a private conversation. Or he might give you a vague direction, like, "I want you to take more initiative." But when you go ahead and redo the filing system or handle a client's request yourself, he gets furious.

  The best way to handle a Crazy Maker is to take careful notes when given orders, then ask questions to confirm where the boundaries lie, and repeat what you believe he wants you to do. You might also ask again before you act, at least initially. Then, when things go wrong (and they will), refer to your notes, and say politely, "My notes say that you wanted me to do such and such. Did I get that wrong?" Just knowing that you take notes might make him focus more on what he's saying and decrease the chances that he'll deny that he gave you certain instructions.

- ▪ ***The Mood Swinger:*** The Mood Swinger is sometimes full of laughter and good cheer, chattering away about his personal life and joking with you about work. But other times, he doesn't even say good morning, snaps at you when you ask how his weekend was, and vents his rage on you for seemingly inconsequential acts. With the Mood Swinger, you may not know who you're dealing with from moment to moment, which can be very unnerving and keep you off balance.

Remind yourself that his moods are not your fault! Do your best to stay out of his personal life, laugh at his jokes when he's happy, and steer clear of him when he's irritable. If he yells at you for things that don't make sense or aren't your fault, be assertive and say something like, "I can see that you're angry with me, and I'm not sure why. Can you please explain?" Then use your empathic listening skills to find out how you can avoid trouble the next time. Chances are he'll simply apologize, because it's really *not* about you. (And even if he doesn't, your gentle assertiveness may help prompt more stable communication in the future.)

■ **The Perfectionist:** It's hard to please the Perfectionist, because he is very controlling and sets the bar extremely high. While he certainly desires success, he's even more determined to avoid failure, a negative orientation that makes him anxious and irritable. His nervousness and short temper will affect the way he treats you, making him critical or even punitive. Everything must be done in a certain way, or he blows his stack. But since he may not tell you exactly what is wanted, or his wishes may change abruptly, you're often operating in the dark.

Like the Crazy Maker, the best ways to handle the Perfectionist are to be as supportive and helpful as possible, take careful notes, and confirm instructions before you act. Then pay great attention to detail in your own performance, so there will be fewer mistakes for him to point out. Finally, be sure to express yourself assertively if and when you feel your rights aren't being respected, or he will surely ride roughshod over you.

Problem solving with a difficult boss

You've now been armed with some general techniques for dealing with difficult bosses in everyday situations. But what do you do when big problems and conflicts arise? How do you approach the Grouch when you feel you've been treated disrespectfully? What do you say to the Crazy Maker when you've been unjustly accused of making a major mistake?

When serious problems crop up, here are a few tips for approaching your difficult boss and arriving at a mutually satisfactory solution (and by the way, these are the same tips I teach for solving *all* communication problems in *any* relationship):

- **Don't procrastinate.** It will be tempting to ignore these problems and hope they'll just disappear. Unfortunately, they usually become bigger problems, so you really need to discuss them with your boss ASAP. Difficult bosses often don't think about the consequences when they act, so it will be up to you to call them on their inappropriate behavior when it occurs. I know this will make you nervous. But the opportunity to clear the air and change things for the better will be worth it. If you let things slide, believe me, they will just get worse.

- **Talk to your boss in private.** Any important communication with your boss should be done behind closed doors, where no one else can hear what you say to each other. For both of you, this will eliminate the possibility of public embarrassment and remove the need to save face in front of others.

- *Lay out the facts in a noncritical way.* Take care when presenting the issue to your boss. Remember, he is in the superior position and not accustomed to being called out or criticized by underlings. Keep it short, focus solely on the facts, and keep your emotions at bay. Then calmly state how you would like things to change in the future. If possible, it's a good idea to rehearse what you plan to say with a trusted (nonwork) friend or family member before you deliver your message.

- *Practice empathic listening.* Your boss, like anyone else, has goals, needs, desires, and emotions, although you may not know what they are. Allow him to tell you about these things, if he wants to. The more you know about his point of view, the better you'll understand him personally, and the easier it will be to work together productively.

- *Understand the personality behind the difficult behavior.* Here's a secret shared by many people who have had long, productive relationships with those who are difficult: It's probably *not* about you. If you can figure out what drives your boss's problem behavior, you'll be able to view it more objectively and take it less personally. And that will make it easier to take.

When the problem stems from you

Of course, there's also the possibility that your boss *isn't* the problem. She may be delivering negative feedback or possibly even avoiding you because your performance or attitude isn't up to snuff. So if you come to the realization that *you* might be the problem, don't wait for her to approach you. Periodically ask for feedback on how you're doing and her ideas for ways you can improve, especially if she seems unhappy with you. If you know what's not working, you have the opportunity to make positive changes.

But even if you're generally doing great, sooner or later you're going to make a mistake that you can't immediately reverse. And the mistake just might be a big one. When that happens, whatever you do, *don't try to cover it up or deny that you did anything wrong.* Since ultimately, it's your boss's responsibility to make things right, it's important for her to hear the bad news right away. Waiting will only compound the trouble for both of you. But before you walk into her office to confess, come up with a solution to the problem, one that you can handle yourself, if possible. Then you'll be able to present both the problem and the potential fix at the same time, which might take some of the sting out of it. If you take responsibility for both the mistake *and* the solution, your boss should regard you more favorably than if you just dump the problem in her lap. Either way, be sure to apologize, sum up what you've learned, and assure her that it won't happen again.

Becoming a Presence at Meetings

It may sound simple, but it's true: The course of your career will depend primarily on two things—your performance and the relationships you make. And while your relationship with your boss will be of utmost importance, the bonds you form with colleagues will also be essential. Your ability to cooperate with your co-workers will be crucial, because the working world is all about collaboration. But if you actually *like* each other and get along well—so much the better! And don't forget that some of your colleagues may be key contacts for you down the line, people who will help you move ahead in your career. In short, the importance of forming good relationships with the people you work with just can't be overestimated. And the place you'll most likely meet and get to know them is in meetings.

A lot of people dread meetings, which they think of as boring, tedious time-wasters that carve up their day and keep them from doing their "real" work. You, however, should *welcome* any chance to attend a meeting (no matter how boring or futile it might seem), because meetings are your best chance of becoming known and recognized throughout your company. They offer you a great opportunity to shine and to foster relationships with people who otherwise might never know you exist. So anytime you get the chance to go to a meeting, embrace it!

Group Roles

That being said, before you show your face at a single meeting, you need to prepare. No matter how casual they may seem, meetings are ritualistic gatherings of people who assume definite roles. Some of these roles may be assigned, like the Leader. But others, like the Clarifier or the Balker, are voluntary and habitual—a person may automatically assume a certain role, even if it's not necessary, because the role feels right or matches his personality.

Some of these group roles are positive and will benefit and improve group function, while others are negative and will hinder it. Those in the former category include:

Positive Group Roles

- **The Leader:** The Leader initiates the meeting; defines the topic or problem to be discussed; requests suggestions, ideas, or opinions; and keeps the discussion on track. She also decides when the meeting ends. (Note: For a meeting to succeed, there always needs to be a Leader, whereas the other roles are somewhat optional or arbitrary.)

- **The Clarifier:** The Clarifier asks questions with the goal of making an idea or example more understandable. He also paraphrases other people's thoughts, objections, or conclusions using language that's easier for others to comprehend. He says things like, "So what I think you're saying is … "

and "It seems that we all agree that … " He helps ensure that everybody understands and agrees on a given point so the group can progress.

■ **The Gatekeeper:** Always aiming to keep group participation positive and evenly distributed, the Gatekeeper asks for input from those who are quiet, saying things like, "Jamal, what do you think about this?" At the same time, she tries to reign in those who are too dominant, with input like, "So I think we understand how Bethany feels about this problem. How about someone else?"

■ **The Encourager:** This person is sort of a group cheerleader, doling out approval, praise, and reassurance in order to buoy the spirit and confidence of group members. He'll say things like, "Wow, that was a very insightful comment, Marika" or "I think we really got a lot done today."

■ **The Harmonizer:** When tension rises or ideas, opinions, or personalities conflict, the Harmonizer looks for commonality, helps tone down disagreements, and refocuses the discussion in a more positive way. He'll make comments like, "Things are getting a little heated, but I think we can all agree on … "

■ **The Succinct Participant:** The Succinct Participant offers relevant ideas, opinions, or other input in a positive, concise, and respectful manner. She takes her turn, listens to others, and doesn't dominate, but also doesn't feel constrained when she has something worthwhile to contribute.

Whether canoeing across a lake with my family or participating in a meeting at work, I usually fall into the roles of Clarifier and Encourager—they fit who I am. If you think about it, you can probably come up with some positive roles that seem natural for you to assume as well. You may also gravitate toward certain negative roles; ones that hamper group function and impede progress.

The "unhelpful" roles include:

Negative Group Roles

- ***The Dominator:*** Aggressive and controlling, the Dominator takes up more than her share of the group's time putting forth her opinions and ideas. She interrupts others, is resistant to their ideas and input, and generally tries to commandeer the discussion.

- ***The Withdrawer:*** The Withdrawer is psychologically and/or physically removed from the group and doesn't say anything unless he's forced. He may believe that his input is not valued or valuable, or there could be unresolved conflicts that keep him from wanting to participate. Whatever the problem, the Withdrawer does not contribute to the group, or he does so reluctantly.

- ***The Balker:*** Aiming to thwart the progress of the group, the Balker is derisive, disagreeable, and uncooperative. Most likely, resentment, grudges, insecurity, or hurt feelings drive her behavior. Whatever the reason, the Balker is simply not going to play the game and does her best to derail the group's progress.

- ***The Disengaged:*** Bored and probably resentful that he's been called into the meeting, the Disengaged either sits with a like-minded individual and engages in whispered private conversation or spends the bulk of the meeting reading messages on his phone. He contributes little or nothing to the group discussion.

Obviously, your goal in any meeting should be to take on a positive role and shun the negative roles. As a newbie, the negative role that is easiest to slip into is the Withdrawer. You probably won't be expected to say anything for a while, unless you have a fairly elevated position, so it's fine if you lie low during your first few meetings. But don't stay in the silent mode for too long—your failure to add to the discussion might make you appear aloof or low in self-esteem. As soon as possible, get in there and become the kind of group member who makes positive contributions. Your presence and input will be valued.

How to become an excellent group member

Here are a few tips to help you become an excellent group member and a positive presence, once you feel you're ready to participate fully in meetings:

- **Be prepared.** Before the meeting, spend some time thinking about and researching the topic. If there's an agenda, bone up on the topics if you can, or ask others for a briefing. And if you've been sent materials to study ahead of time, read them! (You'd be surprised how many meetings I attend where people clearly have not done their homework.) Write down any relevant questions or comments, and bring them with you to the meeting.

- **Be visible.** Sit as close as you can to the Leader, or wherever the action is. This way, people can't help but see you, even if you're not actively contributing. Then be sure to look sharp, project self-assurance, and stay engaged and attentive throughout the entire meeting.

- **Make your presence known.** Try to make at least one comment during every meeting. It's easier to do this early in the meeting; it gets harder and harder to break out of the passive mode as time goes by. But be sure your comments or questions are worthwhile and memorable. Do your best to contribute in a direct and significant way.

- **Be concise.** When contributing to the discussion, get right to the point and wrap it up quickly. No one wants to listen to a monologue.

- **Don't dominate the discussion.** More than two or three questions or comments during a meeting is probably too many, especially if you're new. Let others have their say too.

- **Be aware of your body language.** Sit up, lean forward, and make eye contact with the person who is speaking. Slumping, leaning back in your chair, or fidgeting will make you appear disengaged.

- **Speak up.** Project your voice so that everyone can hear you, but don't yell.

- **Support others in the group.** Don't criticize anyone for their thoughts or comments. If you want to disagree and offer an alternative suggestion, acknowledge the comment in a positive way, then say something like, "Another possibility is that we could … "

- **Don't get defensive.** If someone contradicts you, stay relaxed and open to what he is saying. Defensiveness will show in your body language or vocal tone and can make you seem uncooperative, angry, or immature. Keep your cool.

- **Establish rapport.** Meetings are a great opportunity to build rapport with others. Use your active listening and mirroring techniques to connect with others.

- **Smile.** It's your million-dollar asset! Just make sure you're smiling at appropriate times.

Getting other people to listen to you

In any group, there will always be a few people who seem to do most of the talking. You've been sitting there in silence for much of the meeting, and now you have something you'd really like to say. But the talkers are dominating, the Leader isn't taking control of the situation, and no one is playing the much-needed role of Gatekeeper. How do you get everyone to stop and listen to you?

For starters, here's what *doesn't* work:

- **Waiting your turn:** You might just sit there forever.

- **Raising your hand and hoping someone will "call on you":** This won't do anything except make you look like a schoolkid.

- **Opening with "I" statements:** (e.g., "I think ... ," "I'd like to add ... ," "I did something like that once ... ") This can make it sound like the previous speaker's thoughts or feelings don't matter and you are now going to insert your own.

- **Speaking loudly and quickly:** This will make you seem nervous and insecure.

- **Saying something that isn't pertinent:** Your comments will just be dismissed, and other group members will be less likely to listen to you next time.

Here's what *does* work:

- **Summarizing the comments made by the previous speaker:** You might say, "Maria really hit the nail on the head when she said ... In addition ... " Then you can insert your insightful, viable contribution.

- **Using assertive body language and vocal tone:** Sit up, make yourself as tall and broad as possible; lay your hands flat on the table, palms down; use your power voice in the lower register; speak intelligently; and radiate confidence.

- **Using enumeration:** Remember way back in the foreword, when I told you how much I like lists? Well, think of enumeration as ticking off a list of points on your fingers (e.g., "First, we need to notify our clients; second, we need to follow up with an email blast; third, we need to … "). This will organize your comments and make them easier for all to follow.

■ ***Establishing a reputation as someone who makes intelligent, accurate, worthwhile contributions:*** Do this repeatedly and people will automatically stop and listen to you whenever you speak.

Since most people are a lot more interested in putting in their two cents than listening to you, it will be up to *you* to get in on the action, or you'll be left behind. Be sure to research and study up on the topic prior to a meeting—you'll be more likely to jump in confidently and become a player, instead of being stuck on the sidelines. Once you gain a reputation as a person who makes worthwhile and valuable contributions, others will want to listen to you. And that's a major way of gaining power and visibility.

Are You Being Passed Over for Promotion?

Throughout this entire book, we've been talking about how to make a positive impression on those around you. At this point, you're well established in your position, and you've managed to make some inroads with the decision makers. You're an excellent employee. You always do what's asked of you and more. You get along with your co-workers. You respect your supervisors. You never miss a deadline. You even singlehandedly landed a humongous new contract for your sales team last January. So why did they pass you over for that promotion last year (and the one the year before)? Well, it could be something *other* than mere work performance.

According to a recent study, conducted jointly by CareerBuilder® and The Harris Poll®, of 2,175 hiring and human resources managers across diverse industries and company sizes, it turns out a whopping 62 percent of those surveyed listed a *negative attitude* and *frequent tardiness* as the top two reasons people get passed over for promotion. And what else will sabotage your advancement? Survey responders listed the following: Using crude language (51%), frequently leaving work early (49%), taking excessive sick days (49%), spreading office gossip (44%), using company time to play around on personal social media sites (39%), and neglecting to clean up after yourself (36%).

At this point, in case you're starting to think the survey responders were being a bit nitpicky, hold on to your (hopefully appropriate in your workplace) hat and read on, because the list continues:

- Piercings outside of traditional ear piercings (32%)

- Attire that is too provocative or too casual for the workplace (27%)

- Visible tattoos (27%)

- Initiating too many non-work-related conversations with co-workers (27%)

- Unprofessional or ostentatious* haircut (25%)

- Unprofessional or ostentatious* facial hair (24%)

- Taking personal calls at work (24%)

- Bad breath (23%)

- Heavy perfume or cologne (21%)

- Taking smoke breaks** (19%)

- Too much makeup (15%)

*"Ostentatious" wasn't defined in the study, but we can probably make an educated guess as to what the survey responders meant.

**Notice that they didn't say "Taking *too many* smoke breaks;" the act of simply "Taking smoke breaks" was seen by some responders as enough to kick you out of the running for a promotion. Need I point out that this is still another great reason not to smoke?

Do you notice something missing from this dauntingly long list? Nowhere did anyone mention "poor work performance"! And why would that be? Well, we have to assume that *stellar* work performance is an obvious key criterion for promotion and that *poor* work performance would automatically kick you out of the running, right? So I believe this study is telling us something very important: Exemplary work performance should simply be a given in your advancement strategy, but it's the more subtle stuff you need to pay attention to when you're looking to be promoted.

So, for starters, show up on time (dare I say, "Duh"?), and then, make sure you're displaying that glowing, positive attitude you mastered back in chapter 2. Next, review this list of peccadilloes and see whether you might benefit by making a change or two when it comes to your professional image and work behavior. Remember, whether it's fair or not, *everything* about you—what you say, what you do, how you look, and even how you smell— represents *you* and is fair game for evaluation by your superiors.

Networking the Old-fashioned Way

Becoming powerful and influential takes time, energy, effort, self-discipline, smarts, confidence, and—most of all—good relationships with others, especially people who have power and influence themselves. Social networking is an excellent tool for getting in touch with people you might never have met otherwise (and I suggest you learn all you can about social networking in order to position yourself favorably with this vitally important medium), but nothing carries the impact of real-life, face-to-face meet-ups. These don't necessarily have to be formal meetings. In your workplace, chat with as many people as possible to make yourself known. Offer help to anyone who needs it, without expecting anything in return.

Next, you can broaden out: Attend social events and meetings for people in your particular business, industry, or area of expertise. Ask co-workers, friends, and acquaintances to introduce you to others who might be of help to you or who might need your help. Then, whenever you make a new contact, follow up immediately with an email. If it seems appropriate, try to schedule a time to meet that person for a specific purpose that will be of interest to him or her (coffee, a meal, a game of tennis, and so on). One of your most important goals should be to get out there and get connected, to become seen and known.

We've all heard the saying "It's who you know that counts." Well, here's another take on it: "It's *not only* who you know that counts ... it's also who knows *you*." So become a positive and highly visible presence in your workplace, your business, your industry, and your community, and you're almost sure to travel far in your career.

CHAPTER 9

THE FINE ART OF MANAGING

Let's say you've been working in your current position for a while and all has gone well. You've proven that you're smart, focused, motivated, able to work well with others, and an overall excellent employee. And the powers that be have now decided to promote you to a managerial position! While you're thrilled at the prospect, you're wondering what, exactly, will be expected of you. Will you need to acquire a whole new set of skills? How should you conduct yourself? Will your co-workers be willing to take orders from you, now that you're "the boss"? Or will they ignore you, defy you, or maybe even laugh in your face?

Morphing from worker to manager can be tricky, especially when you suddenly find yourself supervising people who used to be your peers. I know this for a fact since I did it twice: Going from psychiatric aide to clinical director of Crestwood Hospitals and from speaker/trainer to vice president of faculty, curricula, and publications at National Seminars, each in just a few short years. Once you become a manager, you might find that some people are slow to accept you in your new role, while others actively resent you and resist following your lead. But here's what I found is the key to turning them around: What they're waiting for—what they really *need*—is for you to establish your credibility. Before they can function as cooperative, productive employees, they need to believe that you're truly worthy of leading them.

Credibility is the quality of being believable, trustworthy, reliable, and true. It underlies every single thing you say, think, feel, and do. If you're a credible person, you show good judgment and foresight. You're dependable. Your motives are pure and your actions transparent. People don't have to wonder where you're coming from or what you're after; you lay it out in the open for all to see. You don't lie, cheat, steal, or operate in a shady way (I hope that's obvious). When you have credibility, your employees believe in your abilities, judgment, honesty, and good intentions. They feel confident that you're looking out for them and unlikely to steer them in the wrong direction. And that makes it possible for them to commit wholeheartedly to your ideas, plans, and course of action and to perform their own jobs with enthusiasm and confidence.

But if you're lacking in credibility, chaos reigns. People either stop following you or do so half-heartedly. Anger, resentment, resistance, and stagnation begin to spread. Your employees wonder where they're going, what they're doing, and why; out-and-out rebellion is a distinct possibility. In short, when you, as a manager, are short on credibility, nothing much gets done, and the workplace atmosphere can easily become poisonous. Without credibility, you simply can't be an effective leader.

This means your first objective as a new manager *must* be to build your credibility. And once you've built it, you must maintain it every single day for the rest of your career.

Building and Maintaining Credibility

Your credibility *stems from* the way you conduct yourself every minute of every day. It's not something you can paste on when the occasion calls for it; you have to *live* it. Since you've been promoted to a management position, it's clear that you've already accumulated a good amount of credibility—at least as an employee. But now, as you take on the responsibilities of guiding and supervising others, you'll need to expand upon it. To build, strengthen, and improve your credibility, you must:

- **Be honest and ethical.** Strong moral principles and core values should underlie everything you do; they will help you make decisions that are best for everyone. Always strive to do the right thing, even when it's hard, and even when no one else is watching. Know and follow the rules for proper behavior, especially within your profession. And remember that you set the tone; if you are dishonest or ignore the rules from time to time, others will follow suit.

- **Communicate.** Express yourself assertively, and be as clear as possible in all of your communications. Every day, let your employees know what's on your mind and what you expect; then give them opportunities to ask questions or give feedback. Listen more than you speak, and do your very best to keep the lines of communication open. Don't just bark out orders and expect others to comply; use your assertiveness skills to build positive working relationships with everyone around you.

- **Be decisive.** As a manager, you'll be called upon to make endless decisions. Think things through carefully, listen to or review all sides of the issue, and then decide which way you want to go. Trust yourself, your judgment, and your gut feelings, and announce your decision with confidence and clarity. You may need to explain your reasoning (briefly), but then move on. If others balk, you must stand your ground and forge ahead.

- **Be consistent.** When you make promises, keep them. When you set rules, live by them. Don't say one thing, and then do another or give an order, change your mind, and expect your employees to read your thoughts and do something else. If you review your goals before you assign tasks or projects, you'll be less likely to change directions midstream.

■ **Follow up.** Check to see if the assignments you've given have been completed correctly and on time. If you let this slide, it's a sure thing that certain boring or unpleasant tasks will never get done—your employees will assume you'll never notice. Clearly explain any rules to your employees up front. Then have a system in place for dealing with those who break the rules, beginning with gentle reminders and escalating to verbal and written warnings. Address any violations or undesirable behavior immediately; it only gets harder if you wait.

Credibility Destroyers

No matter how much credibility you may have accumulated, you can quickly demolish it by doing any of the following:

■ **Being dishonest or unethical:** This is the fastest way to obliterate your employees' trust and respect. Be above board in all your dealings.

■ **Saying one thing and doing another:** It's fine to set high standards for others, but if you're not willing to practice what you preach, others will disrespect and resent you.

■ **Waffling:** First you say one thing, then you reverse your position, then you ask others what they think you should do. If you're not sure what you want, why should anyone follow you? Figure out what you want and stick with it.

■ *Failing to follow up:* This sends a clear message to your employees that they can get away with any kind of behavior. They'll think you don't really care whether they stick to the rules and complete their assignments—or not. Stay on top of things.

■ *Swearing:* Besides being unpleasant and unprofessional, using foul language makes you appear ill-mannered, crude, or out of control—or all three. Keep it clean.

■ *Associating with unethical people:* You'll be judged (and influenced) by the company you keep. Stay away from shady characters.

■ *Gossiping:* Passing on rumors about others can make you seem insecure, immature, and untrustworthy. It can also damage reputations, including yours. Surely you've got better things to talk about!

■ *Lacking refinement:* Being crude, vulgar, and loud; telling lewd jokes; or otherwise lacking good taste in your speech, gestures, or appearance will lower your standing in the eyes of others and interfere with your message. Always be professional, honorable, and polite.

■ *Communicating in a passive style:* Allowing others to dominate you makes you appear weak, unsure of yourself, and not up to the job. Use basic assertive statements in all of your communications.

- **Communicating in an aggressive style:** Riding roughshod over others not only destroys your credibility, but also breeds resentment and a lack of cooperation. (Ditto for using a passive-aggressive style.) Model what you want to see in others by communicating assertively. Not only is it the right thing to do, but it will earn you the respect and affection of your employees and make everything run much more smoothly.

To build and maintain your credibility, you need to be your "best self" at all times—honest, ethical, clear, consistent, goal-oriented, empathic, and inspiring. You must set an example for others, and be the kind of person who inspires confidence. You must take charge with assurance and sensitivity, and refrain from being a bully. Never forget that you're in charge because you *should* be—you've proven yourself. And in time, even the naysayers will come to appreciate your credibility and be willing (and happy) to follow you.

The 10 Golden Rules of Good Management

Although there are some people who suddenly become very self-important once they make the leap into management (I'm sure we've all met a few!), managing isn't about strutting around like a king surrounded by servants who attend to your every need. Instead, it's more of a symbiotic relationship: Each party needs the other to get the job done. You, as a manager, have certain goals to reach, and your employees have the power to help you achieve those goals. Your end of the bargain is to provide them with direction, encouragement, and whatever they need to get the job done. Their end of the bargain is to do the work. Combining the energies of both parties should result in a win-win situation for all.

Of course, there's a lot more to being a manager than simply setting goals and urging your employees to reach them. *You* must communicate clearly what you want done. *You* must motivate and inspire your employees, and check to see that the work is done correctly and efficiently. *You* must make the decisions, large and small, that steer your employees in a certain direction. And, ultimately, *you* must take responsibility for whatever occurs. Does it all sound a bit overwhelming? It can be.

Knowing this, I've come up with 10 Golden Rules of Management; guidelines that will help you manage others in a kind, firm, assertive, effective manner.

1. ***Treat your employees with respect.*** Respect means knowing and using your employees' names, listening to their concerns regarding their jobs, communicating with them regularly, making sure that they get the training and supplies they need to do their jobs, and helping them find a fair balance between work and personal life. Respecting your employees is worth doing simply because it's right, but it can also benefit you. They will be more cooperative, perform better, work harder, and like you more. They will also be more likely to help you out when you're in a bind—for example, when you need people to come in over the weekend or work late or otherwise go above and beyond the call of duty. (And believe me, that day will definitely come for you as a manager.)

2. ***Keep your goals at the forefront.*** Along with continuously monitoring your short-term and medium-term goals for both you and your work group, several times a day, remind yourself of what you're trying to accomplish *in the long run.*

Goals like "We want to provide the best client service in the industry" or "We want to be hippest, most cutting-edge company in our field" will help you put things in perspective and guide you toward correct decisions.

3. **Be a role model.** Your behavior will be noticed and emulated by your employees, for better or for worse. Be a living example of the kind of person you'd like your employees to be. They're always observing you, whether you realize it or not.

4. **Engage.** Don't spend the day glued to your chair behind closed doors. Get around and be visible in your department. Check in with your employees; chat a little and ask how things are going. Then be ready and willing to listen to problems, ideas, or concerns. When employees come to you with trouble, don't cut them off, give pat answers, rush off to a meeting, or tell them to handle it themselves—the problem will only grow. Stay positive, recognize and deal with any negativity, and work with them to come up with problem-solving strategies. Then be sure to follow up to see if further steps need to be taken.

5. **Tailor your approach to the individual.** Always remember that you're dealing with human beings—unique individuals with their own thoughts, feelings, desires, and experiences—not widgets. So a one-size-fits-all approach to dealing with your employees isn't going to cut it. For example, some people may do fine with quick, direct instructions, while others need more prompting, and still others need to know the rationale behind your choices. It's important that you get to know your employees personally in order to gain insight into how best to approach each one.

6. **Be brief.** Keep your requests, updates, and explanations short and to the point. If it takes you a long time to explain what you want, you probably haven't thought it through well

enough. Ask yourself: What's the bottom line? What's really important? Then come up with a message that is concise, clear, and accurate. Your employees (and everyone else in your life) will be much more likely to understand what you expect of them and why.

7. **Encourage ideas and opinions.** Your employees can be a great source of innovative and practical ideas. Someone might come up with a fantastic new way to promote a product, arrange the storeroom, appeal to clients, or make a better pot of coffee. Always encourage input from your employees on any topic. Let them know that your door is always open and you want to know what's on their minds. You may find a new answer to an old problem, and your employees will feel more empowered and involved.

8. **Accept personal responsibility.** Don't try to hide your own errors, unless you can correct them immediately without affecting anyone or anything. If you make a mistake (and, of course, you will), admit it to all who are affected, apologize, and explain how you will make amends. Don't ever blame your employees for departmental mishaps. It's your job to ensure that each employee performs her job correctly and responsibly, so if someone messes up, it's on you. Own it, fix it, and move on.

9. **Be inspiring.** Long ago I heard the story of a janitor who worked at an aviation plant during World War II. Although he spent his days mopping floors and cleaning toilets, when he was asked what he did for a living, he replied, "I'm helping to win the war." No matter which tasks he was doing, the janitor realized he was contributing to a larger purpose in an important way. Help your employees feel the same way by appreciating their contributions, pointing out how they helped achieve departmental goals, encouraging them

when they're down, and inspiring them to do their best at all times. And be sure to recognize them when they do something especially well.

10. **Make your workplace fun.** Remember way back in chapter 1 when I said that one of our founding goals for SkillPath was to have fun? This idea really worked for us; we had a happy, cohesive, hardworking group, most of whom stayed at SkillPath for years, and many of whom are still there 28 years later. If your workplace atmosphere is light and relaxed, everyone will have more fun and find it more pleasurable to go to work. You can set the tone by being enthusiastic and happy about what you're doing. Then allow your employees to create their own fun—make it okay for them to talk, laugh, and visit as long as the work gets done. If somebody wants to organize potlucks or birthday celebrations (it doesn't have to be you), let the fun happen—and always participate!

These 10 Golden Rules of Management are all about how to treat others and model good behavior. But here's a "rule" that's specifically for you: Believe in yourself. You were brought on as a manager for a reason; someone could see that you had the right stuff. And you do. So trust your own judgment and go with it. Only one person can steer the ship effectively, and that person is *you*.

How to Treat Your Assistant

Quite often, one of the perks and necessities of being a manager is having an assistant to handle your phone calls, schedules, filing, and endless office details. Your assistant is more than just a helper. He's part of your professional image, the first person to answer your phone or greet your visitors, the one who makes arrangements in your name, and a primary representative of you and your office.

If you have an excellent assistant, your life will be easier. You'll be kept informed, your office and work output will be well organized, and you'll be able to access what you need when you need it. But if you have a poor assistant, your life can get harder. You may find yourself constantly on edge, wondering what's being done in your name, whether tasks are being completed properly (or at all), worrying about missed messages, and waiting for disasters to occur because of incompetence or communication breakdowns.

While most assistants fall somewhere between excellent and poor, here's a tip for you: You can improve the level of service you get from your assistant just by treating that person well. That's because he, like other employees, gets to decide how hard he's going to work for you. He can do the bare minimum (while still hanging on to his job) or go the whole nine yards to make things just about perfect. Or he can do something in between. Because your assistant's performance can do so much to make you look great (or like a bumbling idiot), it makes good sense to cultivate an excellent relationship with him. Here are some good ways to do so:

- **Be sincerely cordial and friendly.** You don't have to be best friends with your assistant. In fact, if you become overly chummy, it could become difficult to maintain the proper boss-employee alliance. But it's essential that the two of you have a positive working relationship, and forging a true friendship is certainly within the realm of possibility (actually, many of my former assistants have become my lifelong friends). So minimally, always be sure to say "good morning" and "good-bye," smile, ask a friendly question or two (e.g., "How was your weekend?"), and treat him as a fellow human being.

- **Always say "please" and "thank you."** This applies to all requests that you make, no matter how big or small.

- **Ask politely.** Just because you're in the position of giving instructions doesn't mean you get to shout them out like a drill sergeant. When making a request, try phrasing it as a question, as in, "Can you get Jack Ahmad on the line, please?" Your assistant will understand that it's a request, not a question. But it's so much more pleasant than, "Get me Jack Ahmad!"

- **Use his name respectfully.** It's nice to precede a request with the person's name, as in, "Brian, I have something I'd like you to take to the mail room." However, yelling "Brian!" 50 times a day is going to make him irritable and resentful.

- **Use the intercom instead of calling out orders.** If your assistant sits outside your office or cubicle, you may be tempted to shout requests as they come to mind. Don't. It's noisy and annoying, and you'll be heard by others in the office. Use the intercom or instant messaging; that's why they were invented.

- **Don't ask him to handle your personal chores.** Unless these tasks are discussed up front as part of the job, don't ask your assistant to pay your bills, pick up your dry cleaning, plan your nonbusiness parties, or walk your dog. He's not your personal slave.

- **Keep him informed about what you're doing.** The more your assistant knows, the more interested he'll be in his job and the better he can serve you. Briefly explain what you're working on, what your goals are, and what's important to you. You'll find he'll be more efficient when scheduling your appointments, more adept at anticipating your needs, and more informed about what to say (and what not to say) to others. If you keep your assistant in the dark, he can make serious on-the-job mistakes and easily become a bored, disengaged employee.

- **Express your thanks in a special way.** A few times a year, tell your assistant how much his help means to you. Christmas/Hanukkah, his birthday, and Administrative Professionals Day are good times to do this, although you could choose other times throughout the year as well. You don't have to give him anything expensive, but a small gift, plus a handwritten note, will be appreciated and make him more likely to go the distance for you.

One last thing: Even though you're the boss, remember that you and your assistant are equal on a human level, and he should always be treated with respect, loyalty, and dignity. It all boils down to three things: Being polite, not taking advantage, and showing some appreciation—nothing spectacular or difficult. Still, you'd be surprised at how many managers treat their assistants in a careless, inconsiderate manner. In the long run, this comes back to haunt them in the form of a poorly run office and a revolving door of assistants. Do yourself a favor and don't be one of those bosses. Take the time to ensure that your relationship with your assistant remains positive, productive, and enjoyable. It will be worth the effort.

"Instructive Talking"— How to Give Feedback

Like it or not, as a manager, you will need to have talks with your employees about their behavior on a regular basis. In fact, one of your most important tasks will involve observing your employees and making mental notes about their performance, teamwork, level of interest and commitment, and so on. Then you'll need to give them feedback about what you see, especially if it looks like a problem may be developing.

Feedback, which is sometimes referred to as "instructive talking," is communicating comments, opinions, or messages to another person about her behavior. In the best of all worlds, feedback provides an employee with a clear reflection of how her behavior is affecting both her performance and other people, for better or for worse. This means that feedback can be positive or negative.

Although pointing out others' mistakes and telling them how to improve may seem to be essential to improving performance, I've found that giving positive feedback can be even more important. When good behavior is noticed and appreciated, people become more confident, committed, and interested in their jobs. They're also more likely to repeat the behavior. I've learned to make a point of giving an employee positive feedback whenever I see that she's done a good job, helped someone else succeed, or functioned well as a team member. It always makes things even better!

Of course, I'm not saying that you can skip out on giving negative feedback. When an employee is slacking off, doing a poor job, or not cooperating with others, you have to let that person know what you've observed, how it impairs progress, and the effect it has on those around her. But you can't stop there: You'll need to help her find ways to make a change. Giving negative feedback is like holding up a mirror to another person so she can see what she's doing and figure out ways to improve. Here's what it's *not*: Scolding, threatening, haranguing, nagging, punishing, or preparing an employee to get the boot. When you give feedback (whether it's negative or positive), you're offering her a learning experience.

Keep these two important rules in mind whenever you give feedback—positive or negative: Be specific and don't delay.

- **Be specific.** First, focus on the action or task, rather than on the employee herself, then give explicit details. For example, instead of saying, "Kyla, you're a great accountant!" say, "Kyla, I'm so impressed with the way you pulled all the numbers together and got this report out so quickly. Thank you!" Or, instead of saying, "Jayden, you don't seem committed enough to do this project the way I need it done," say, "Jayden, thanks for your hard work on this project, although I was hoping it would be done last week. Any ideas for helping to speed up the process?" In each case, the employee has a clear idea of what went right or wrong because the feedback was specific and precise.

- **Don't delay.** Here's an interesting behavioral fact: The sooner you provide feedback to an employee (or to anyone, for that matter) after a behavior has occurred, the more likely it is that learning will take place. Feedback is most effective when you deliver it right away, when an incident is still fresh in everyone's minds. Don't wait until the yearly evaluation rolls around before you tell an employee that you noticed he was late to work five times the previous March. (He probably thought you didn't care!) Similarly, when an employee puts together a priority project in record time, compliment him on his efficiency right away. Otherwise, he'll think you didn't appreciate his gargantuan effort.

The exception to this rule is when you need to give negative feedback but you're still gathering information and deciding on your approach. This is a necessary step, so be sure you complete it. Just don't let too much time slip by before you address the matter.

Seven steps for dealing with problem behavior

If you're like most people, you want to be liked and thought of as a nice person. You relish peace and harmony and will go out of your way to avoid conflict. But when things go awry or employees don't perform the way they should, you, the manager, must step in to get things back on course.

For example, let's say you have an employee, Ethan, who has missed several deadlines for submitting reports. He has also forgotten to order sufficient paper for the copy machine more than once and seems generally uninterested and unmotivated on the job. His co-workers have complained to you about constantly having to borrow paper from another department. Then someone tells you that Ethan was recently spotted sleeping on the job. You need to handle this *now*. There are seven steps that can help you deal with problem behavior speedily, efficiently, and with grace. Here's what to do:

1. ***Gather information.*** Resist the urge to act before you understand the situation fully. You may think you know what the problem is, but there could be mitigating circumstances. Observe Ethan in action. Check his work record and find out exactly how many deadlines he has missed. Ask Ethan's co-workers privately about the number of times they've run out of copier paper. Interview the person who saw Ethan sleeping on the job. Be sure you have a clear picture of the situation before you do anything else.

2. ***Think through what you want to say.*** Figure out your objectives before you bring Ethan in for a talk. One objective should be to understand Ethan's side of the story. You also need to figure out exactly what you want from Ethan: To complete his work on time? To order copier paper in a timely way? To become more invested in his job? To stay awake at his desk? Choose only those that you can insist on realistically. Getting Ethan to change his attitude or point of view (e.g., become more invested in the job) will be practically impossible. Instead, stick to behavioral objectives.

3. ***Focus on the unwanted behavior, instead of personal characteristics.*** Bring Ethan in for a face-to-face meeting in your office, and explain the problem in a factual manner. Do not attack him as a person. You might say, "Ethan, I've noticed that you missed three deadlines in the last month, and your colleagues told me they ran out of copier paper

twice during the last month. There have also been reports that you were asleep at your desk recently." *Don't* say, "Gee, Ethan, it seems like you're pretty unmotivated and uninterested" or "Are you getting lazy on me?" Focus on the facts and leave personality out of it.

4. ***Be understanding.*** Once you've laid out the facts, give Ethan a chance to explain himself. Perhaps his mother is in the hospital and he's been up nights worrying about her. Maybe he's going through a divorce. Maybe another employee is bullying him and his response has been to retreat. Try to understand Ethan's side of the story.

5. ***Create a solution with your employee.*** At this point, restate your objectives. Tell Ethan exactly what you need from him, as in, "I need you to complete those reports by the end of business every Friday. I need you to make sure we always have sufficient paper for the copy machine. And I need you to stay awake at your desk at all times." Then, work with him to find ways that will help him succeed. If Ethan's problems stem from personal troubles, perhaps his workload could be lightened temporarily. He may need help in budgeting his time more effectively. Perhaps it's as simple as increasing the number of cartons of paper he orders and making a point of ordering on the first of each month. Whatever the problem, if Ethan is involved in finding the solution, he'll be much more likely to comply.

6. ***Set goals and deadlines.*** Each solution must also include goals and deadlines; otherwise the talk you've just had with Ethan will be just that—talk. Lay out a timetable for achieving measurable goals. You might say, "Now that I've reduced your workload, I will expect all of your reports to be on my desk by 5 p.m. each Friday."

7. **Follow up and review progress.** At the end of your meeting with Ethan, set a time to review his progress and assess the effectiveness of your solutions by saying, "Let's meet again next Friday so you can tell me how things are going." Then follow up at least twice. If all seems to be going well, you can assume the problem has been solved. But if any problems persist, you may need to start again at step one.

Crying

Let's say you've brought an employee into your office, and you're trying to tell her how you'd like her to change her behavior. Then, suddenly, she bursts into tears. Yikes—now what? Having dealt with many criers during my career, I can tell you it's never easy. But I've learned a few things along the way about dealing with tears and those who shed them.

First, there are two kinds of criers: The sincere and the manipulative. Sincere criers are naturally emotional people who have difficulty controlling their tears. They cry easily about lots of things; that's just the way they are. (I can sometimes be a sincere crier—just show me a YouTube® video with puppies in it! I also cried both times when I met a giraffe—and I don't even think I can explain why.) The sincere crier's predilection toward tears is basically the same thing seen in others as uncontrollable shaking, blushing, or sweating—it just happens. Manipulative criers, on the other hand, *can* control their tears, but have found that people tend to give them more leeway and let them off more easily when they cry. So they turn on the waterworks whenever they feel it may benefit them.

When you're talking to someone who suddenly starts crying, you may find yourself tongue-tied, or at least reluctant to be as candid as you might be otherwise. It can be tempting to let the issue slide, maybe after blurting out, "Well, okay, just never do it again," or worse, "Oh, please don't cry! Let's just forget it ... " But don't. Here's the good news: You never have to try and guess—possibly incorrectly—which type of crier you're dealing with. Whether you encounter a sincere crier or one who's blatantly attempting to manipulate you with tears, your response should be the same: "I know this is difficult for you, but I need to continue." Then proceed. You might pause for a few moments to let the person compose herself (or himself), but then carry on. And guess what? Sincere criers will appreciate that you haven't made a huge deal out of their crying (they usually wish they weren't crying to begin with), while manipulative criers will learn that this method of manipulation doesn't work on you.

And what should you do if *you* tend to be a crier? If you're a manipulative crier, stop. Now. Such behavior is passive-aggressive, and there are assertive ways you can use to achieve your goals that are much better for everyone involved. If you're a sincere crier, do your best to control it. No matter how sincere you might be, it will be extremely hard for others to take you seriously if you break into tears whenever difficult situations arise. People are most likely to cry when blamed for something, snubbed, attacked, insulted, passed over for promotion, laid off, or fired, so if you're faced with any of these situations, it's important that you detach yourself emotionally and remember that you are a strong, competent human being, capable of remaining calm and in control. Stay as professional as possible and be seen as someone who handles difficult situations well. Then later, when you're on your own or with your best friend, you can have a good cry.

If, despite your best efforts to control yourself, you end up crying in a work setting (or any other place you wish you weren't), have a brief, unapologetic statement ready that recognizes your behavior; something like, "Regardless of the fact that I'm crying, I need to continue with this conversation" or "We both realize I'm crying right now, but I have something important to say, and I'm going to continue." Others will respect you for your tenacity, even when the going gets rough. And, as a side benefit, by refusing to let your crying intimidate and own you, these episodes should lessen naturally over time. (By the way, this method also works if you happen to be someone who shakes, blushes, or breaks out in a sweat when you're confronted with a difficult situation: Recognize your behavior briefly and unapologetically, and then press onward.)

Managing Others Is a Learning Experience

There is so much involved in being a good manager that it can't be condensed into one short chapter. You now know enough of the basics to make an excellent start, and endless information on the subject can found via the Internet, books, seminars, and the like. Never stop learning! Of greatest importance are the building and maintaining of your credibility, making sure you understand what your bosses expect from you and your department, following the 10 Golden Rules of Management, keeping the lines of communication open between you and your employees, and dealing effectively with problem behavior. Once you master these strategies, you'll be well on your way to becoming a valuable and effective leader.

CHAPTER 10

WHEN MOVING UP MEANS MOVING ON

L et's face it: The days of the 30-year career at a single company are long gone. And so is the era when a CEO might spy a bright young go-getter in the mailroom, get him into the executive training program, and hand him the reins of the company a few years later. Today, according to the Bureau of Labor Statistics, the average U.S. worker has worked at her current job for just 4.4 years! Thanks to corporate buyouts; mass layoffs; jobs replaced by technology; and the hiring of part-time, freelance, and contract workers, job stability seems to have hit a new low. The problem is made worse by thousands of employees, restless because of a lack of upward mobility and wages that don't keep up with the cost of living, who leave their jobs looking for greener pastures.

This means that chances are excellent you'll end up changing jobs, and maybe even careers, several times during your work life. Sometimes, it won't be your choice. Other times you'll be the one to pull the plug, hopefully because you've found a better position, although it could be for more dire reasons, like preserving your health and sanity. But no matter how it happens, at some point you're probably going to find yourself on the move, in search of another job.

Before You Go: Are Your On-the-Job Demands Realistic?

We live in an age of instant gratification: We want what we want *now*! And, more often than not, we get it. Texting, Instagram®, shopping on the Internet, drive-through restaurants, Keurig® coffee makers, same-day delivery (by drones!), and the ability to get immediate answers from Google® to any question imaginable are all part of our everyday lives. Delayed gratification may seem like an old-school, annoying, tedious approach to reaching your career goals—after all, it can take weeks, months, years, and even decades before you get what you're after. But, trust me, more often than not, that's the way it works.

Delayed gratification means putting off what you want today in favor of getting something better down the line, often *way* down the line. For example, you work out at the gym today so you'll be in better physical shape in the future. You forgo dinners out and fancy vacations for years so you can buy a house one day. You take classes at the local community college so you can get your real estate license by the end of the year. There are no quick or easy ways to reach any of these goals; you've simply got to invest and wait for returns.

The same principles apply to building a career. When you're just starting out, you might still be in the instant gratification mode that's worked so well for you in other areas of your life. You might think you deserve praise for showing up at work regularly and doing everything you're supposed to do—and certainly for exceeding the normal job requirements. You may expect your job to be pleasant, and even fun, most of the time. You may assume that as long as you do a good job, you'll get regular raises and periodic promotions. And you may think that your employer will understand that your personal life needs to come first, at least some of the time.

Reality check: It's highly possible that *none* of these things are going to happen. Instead, you may have to work at some pretty boring, un-fun jobs, for people who primarily notice what you do wrong. You most likely won't see a raise for at least a year, and you may never get a promotion. Oh, and your boss will probably assume that your *job*—not your personal life—should be your first priority.

That's when your ability to delay gratification has to kick in. Constantly remind yourself that you're building a career, which takes time, effort, commitment, and patience. You'll have to praise yourself (silently) for the things you do right, because your boss may simply expect you to perform that way. You might not move ahead at every place you work for several reasons: There may be nowhere to go, there may be very few senior positions in the company (no matter how much of a superstar you are), or the owner may be dead set on hiring his relatives. Remind yourself that you're there to gain experience, increase your understanding of the business, and make contacts (remember networking?). Learn everything you can, forge as many relationships as possible, work hard, and stay positive. Then, when it's feasible, move on to another position. Delayed gratification is tough, but it works.

When Leaving Is *Your* Choice

I definitely don't recommend walking away from a job until you're sure that it's a lost cause. Jobs are hard to come by, and the risks that come with leaving can be high. Unless you're immediately going to another position with comparable pay and benefits, you'll have to contend with a drop in income and, possibly, a lapse in insurance. If your departure is resented, you may damage relationships that you've made on the job. There's also the problem of your résumé—jumping from one job to another in a short amount of time can make you look flighty and unreliable to prospective employers. So, before you give your job the heave-ho, make sure you have some pretty darn good reasons for leaving.

Viable reasons for leaving a job

The absolute best reason for leaving a job is to take a different one that's more attractive. Perhaps it's a higher position, or it's in an area (or even a brand-new field) that interests you. Perhaps it offers you an increase in salary and/or benefits or shorter hours so you'll have more time to spend with your family. Or perhaps you want to leave to start up your own business. (Check out the Entrepreneurship section near the end of this chapter.)

Whatever the reasons, if you're really excited about this new position and it looks like a step up, take it. Even if it doesn't turn out to be everything you hoped it would be, you'll learn new skills, form new relationships, and develop in new ways.

However, sometimes you may need to leave a job not for some fantastic opportunity, but because it's blocking your career progress or has become detrimental to you physically or psychologically. I believe it's completely reasonable (and even advisable) to pack your stuff and say good-bye when you find yourself in the following situations:

- You work for a person or a company you know to be corrupt
- You work for a person who constantly criticizes you or beats you up psychologically
- You work for a person who is a substance abuser, mentally unstable, or truly incompetent
- Your salary is too low to support you, your family, and/or your desired lifestyle
- Your work schedule is so demanding that you have no time to do anything else
- Your workload has increased, yet your pay has stayed the same
- Your job is adversely affecting your health
- You really can't stand your boss and/or the people you work with
- You dread going to work every day
- You constantly dream about doing something else for a living
- There are no opportunities for advancement, yet you want to rise
- The company culture is a bad fit for you
- The company politics have changed and become detrimental to you

Whether you're thinking of leaving your job for a great new position or to extricate yourself from a bad situation, it's important to do some soul-searching before you make your decision. Start by making a list of the pros and cons of your current job. What do you like about it? Surely there are *some* things—the people, the money, the time off, the hours? Then zero in on exactly what's bugging you about the job. Can you boil it down to one or two items? While one or two annoying problems can make an entire situation seem untenable, your job may be salvageable by making just a couple of fixes. Once you've written down all the pros and cons you can think of, review the list. Are there more pros or more cons? Are the cons fixable? What would it take to keep you in this job?

Once you've figured out what you really want and need from your current job, have a heart-to-heart talk with your boss. Be polite, assertive, and clear. Lay out the problems you've experienced and describe the changes you'd like to see. If you've been offered another job, you're in a great position to negotiate: Either your current company matches (or exceeds) what the new company is offering, or you're gone. As long as you use this method judiciously, honestly, and nonthreateningly, this is one of the most common and effective ways to advance through the corporate ranks. (However, be cautious with this method: It should be used sparingly, and only when you truly intend to leave, or you'll develop a reputation of being an unscrupulous schemer.)

Even if you don't have this kind of leverage, you'll come away from this talk with a clearer picture of your standing in the company and your chances of advancing. Although you may not be offered more money or a different position, it's possible that some of the "cons" on your list will be resolved as a result of your discussion. Or—providing the conversation went well—your boss may quietly begin looking for a better job match for you within the company.

But let's say you can't stand the work you're doing, can't tolerate your boss, and don't like most of the people in your department. There are way too many problems to be solved by a candid conversation with your boss (especially since she is part of the problem). Still, before you throw up your hands and walk out the door, take advantage of your status as a company insider. Contact HR and ask about job opportunities in other departments or training programs you might be able to join. Ask everyone you know about opportunities they may know of within their departments or elsewhere. Someone might steer you to an open position (inside the company or out) that would be just right for you—and even recommend you for it. It's certainly worth a try.

Finally, ask yourself if leaving this job will bring you a clear return on investment. If you're just walking away and hoping you'll find something down the road, you might end up unemployed far longer than you ever imagined. And you may be forced to take a job that's even less appealing than this one. Don't be rash—before you throw your job away, make sure you're going to be better off without it.

If you've decided that you really have to go ...

Okay, you've carefully weighed the pros and cons of leaving your job. You've spoken with your boss about the problems you've experienced at work, but nothing has changed. You've looked for opportunities in your current company, and none of them appeal to you, or there aren't any at all. Now you've come to the conclusion that you'll be better off leaving both your job and the company. If you're lucky or resourceful enough to have another position lined up, go ahead and accept it, and find out how soon they want you to start. (Skip to the next section, "Making a gracious exit.")

If you don't have another job lined up, you'll have to decide whether to quit now and start hunting for a job once you're unemployed or search for another position while keeping your current one. Experts will tell you that the employed *always* stand a better chance of getting hired than the unemployed, and I agree with this. I'm far more comfortable hiring a person who's logically and calmly conducting a job search than one who's desperately looking to make next month's rent. Still, the logistics of conducting a job search while you're still working can be tricky. For starters, how much should you tell your boss? If you flat-out announce that you're looking for another job, he just might tell you to start packing *now*. But if you keep it a secret, how do you discreetly handle phone calls from prospective employers and get time off to go to interviews?

Whenever possible, I believe it's best to keep your job search private. Don't tell anyone what you're doing, including your best friend, especially if there's the slightest chance that it might get back to your boss. (And it might; this is the kind of gossip that spreads like wildfire.) Use your cell phone, not your work phone, to speak to prospective employers, and handle these calls on your breaks or before/after work hours. Try to arrange several interviews on the same day, then take the entire day off from work. While I am not one to suggest telling fibs, in a pinch, you might need to say you have a personal appointment (implying doctor, dentist, car repairs, or something similar) so you can run off to an interview. Just be aware that using this excuse too many times will arouse suspicions.

Making a gracious exit

Whether you're leaving your job because you've found a better position or you just can't take another day, it's oh-so-important to leave on a positive note. Do your utmost to make a good impression on one and all as you exit. The contacts you've made there may be valuable sources of information, jobs, or referrals down the line, so you don't want to ruffle any feathers if at all possible. You may also end up working with or for some of these people someday, especially if your industry is small. Or you may find yourself returning to this company—it happens more often than you think! So, to the best of your ability, be the kind of person they would welcome back with open arms.

With this in mind, no matter how exuberant, impatient, fed up, relieved, resentful, or happy you may feel on the way out the door, be a living example of a team player and class act by doing the following:

- **Tell your boss you're leaving before you tell anyone else at work.** Your boss will most likely feel disrespected and think less of you if he hears of your plans through the grapevine. Grant him the courtesy of hearing it from you first, and include why you're leaving and when. Once he understands that you're truly serious, he might come up with a very attractive offer that persuades you to stay. If not, at least he will respect your decision and the way you conduct yourself.

- **Give at least two weeks' notice.** This is the standard amount of time employees agree to stay on after announcing their intention to leave. But if your employer is truly left in the lurch with just two weeks' notice, you might agree to stay on a little longer. Don't hang in there for more than a month, however. You may discover that you're treated like a cast-off shoe. Or you may lose your resolve and end up staying indefinitely. It's also possible that your employer will ask you to leave the day you resign and, if so, don't take it personally—it may be company policy. However, if you're asked to leave immediately, know that it's customary, but not mandatory, for employees to be paid for the full two-week period—yet another reason not to ruffle feathers upon your departure.

- **Tie up loose ends.** A lot of employees (possibly most of them) completely lose interest in the job on their way out and leave things in a mess for their replacements. Don't do it. Be the kind of person who leaves things in better shape than she found them. Finish as many projects as possible, clean out your files, box up old materials for storage, and leave the place in good working order. If for no other reason, you should do it as a courtesy to your replacement.

- *Offer to help train your replacement.* This person deserves to start on a level playing field, so no matter how you may feel about the job or the company, help her get established. You know all the ins and outs of the job, so be a sport. Don't make her figure everything out by herself. It's quite simply the decent thing to do.

- *If asked, agree to participate in an exit interview.* Exit interviews are usually conducted by a representative of the HR department. You will be asked to evaluate, either orally or in writing, your overall experience at the company, and you might also be asked to evaluate your boss, your co-workers, the working environment, the company's benefits package—pretty much anything related to the job you're leaving. It's very important to be honest, but it's equally important to remain professional. You already know the difference between delivering constructive feedback to help improve working conditions at the company and bad-mouthing every last aspect of your soon-to-be former job. Be sure to stick to what's helpful and productive.

You might also offer to be available for follow-up questions after you've left the job, although this is optional. It's a pretty safe bet that you won't get many phone calls, so it's an easy way to appear gracious without having to pay a big price. But sometimes you may be called upon because you're the only person who knows where an important piece of equipment was stored or who to contact to get that special cut-rate printing deal. If you can help out, do it.

When Leaving Is *Their* Choice

Losing a job is always tough, no matter what the reason, but sometimes it can't be helped. There are two ways that a company can dismiss you: They can either lay you off or fire you.

You may be laid off because your company has too little work or not enough funds to maintain its current staff and must cut back on its employees. This kind of dismissal has nothing to do with your personal performance, and you might be rehired when business picks up. (In some businesses, layoffs can be seasonal and rehiring happens routinely.)

You may be fired because of unsatisfactory personal performance, a lack of compliance with company standards or policies, publicly embarrassing the company, damaging company property, or failing to adhere to the terms of your employee contract. Most employee contracts are "at-will" agreements, which allow your employer to fire you (or allow you to quit) for any reason at any time. If you've signed such a contract, which you probably did on your original application form, you could theoretically be fired simply because your boss doesn't like you or he thinks you've got an obnoxious laugh. (Don't worry about this too much—we're talking *theoretical* here, and it doesn't usually happen.) However, if you think you are being fired because of your sex, age, race, sexual orientation, religion, disability, or national origin, there may be some legal remedies, depending on your state. While those who are laid off are often rehired, this is almost never the case with those who are fired.

Hopefully, you'll sail through your entire career without ever being laid off or fired. But if you are, I have some definite thoughts about how to make the process easier for all involved. And before I continue, allow me to anticipate your potential response: As you read on, it's quite possible that you'll start to think, "She's *got* to be kidding me! Why would I be so helpful and cooperative if I'm being laid off or fired by this bunch of jerks?" Please trust me here. I've pretty much seen it all, and I promise that remaining professional, positive, and assertive is *always*, without exception, the best way to handle any situation that comes your way, including being laid off or fired. I will say it once again: *Everything* you say and do represents *you!* So in the words of *Anchorman's* Ron Burgundy, "Stay classy ... "

If you're laid off ...

Obviously, being laid off is much easier on the ego than being fired, because it's not your fault. Whatever the reason you're being laid off—whether your company is downsizing, your job has been replaced by technology, or the seasonal workload is at an end—as long as you're not being laid off unfairly or illegally, do the following:

- **Stay positive.** Be the kind of employee the company will want to bring back as soon as possible. Don't complain, cry, gripe, or bad-mouth anyone. The more optimistic and confident you are, the smoother things will go for you.

- **Organize your workload.** Finish your projects, tidy up, and make it as easy as possible for the person who assumes your job duties. Be aware that someone is probably going to be doing double work, so have a heart.

- **Train others and offer to be available for questions by phone.** The smoother the transition, the more you'll be appreciated, and the more likely it will be that you're rehired.

- **Stay in touch.** You'll be the first to hear about reopened positions if you keep in touch with the remaining employees. But don't bug anyone. You want them to want you back!

Even if you've been told that your layoff is temporary, it's important that you don't assume things will work out this way. They may not, so use your time off to network like crazy and look seriously for a new job. With plenty of persistence, you just might find yourself a job that's even better than the last one—and more stable.

A Word About Drawing
Unemployment Benefits ...

Unemployment benefits are an important and valuable safety net designed to provide you with funds when you've lost your job through no fault of your own and you're trying to find a new position. What unemployment is *not* supposed to be is a paid vacation, courtesy of state and federal government policies and your former employer, which serves as a sort of consolation prize for losing your job. Still, some people feel entitled to take a nice long break while collecting unemployment and, once rested, get around to looking for another job.

This is imprudent on a lot of levels, not the least of which is taking resources that other more disadvantaged people might really need. But it's also bad for you personally, especially if you're serious about your career. Drawing unemployment any longer than absolutely necessary will block your career momentum, dull your instincts, and weaken your resolve, and perhaps most importantly, it doesn't look good on your résumé to be away from your career for an extended period of time. And the longer you stay out of the workplace, the more likely you'll be to fall into habits like sleeping late, procrastinating, and taking the easy way out. Obviously, none of these are conducive to career building.

For all of these reasons, it's important that you begin a diligent job search immediately, while you're still fresh from the workplace, and that you rely on unemployment for as short a period as possible. And if you find yourself thinking, "Well, I've always got unemployment, so maybe I'll take a week off from job searching and head to the beach," take it as a sign that your motivation is starting to slide. Instead, strive to become more conscientious, motivated, and goal-oriented than ever.

If you're fired ...

If you should ever find yourself in this unfortunate position, the first thing you'll probably want to do is exactly what you should *not* do—yell, slam doors, call people insulting names, tell anyone who will listen to take this job and shove it, and walk off in a huff. You may also be tempted to delete all the files on your computer, throw out important papers, and bad-mouth your boss and the company to the world. But all of these will just make everything worse. For your own sake, adhere to these dos and don'ts:

Dos

- *Do be polite and respectful at all times.* This is no time to burn bridges. When speaking with your boss, HR representatives, or anyone else at the company, keep your emotions under control and don't be rude or offensive. Remember, these people may be contacted by your future employers. Don't give them any reasons to stick it to you.

- *Do try to keep your composure.* Giving way to angry outbursts, crying, or begging for another chance is just going to make it harder on everybody, including you. Stay as calm and controlled as possible, if only to maintain your dignity.

- *Do get help if you feel you're being discriminated against.* If you truly believe you're being fired because of your sex, age, race, sexual orientation, religion, disability, or national origin, contact the EEOC or Department of Labor. Launching a legal claim against your boss or place of work is a huge deal, and I guarantee it'll be stressful, but sometimes it's warranted.

- **Do start looking for a job right away.** The longer you stay out of the workplace, the harder it will be to get back in. When applying for a new job, always be honest. You don't have to say you were fired; you can say you were "released." However, an interviewer will ask you why, and you should have a well-rehearsed answer like, "It wasn't a good fit for the company or for me" or "It was time to move on."

Don'ts

- **Don't get up and walk out while you're being fired.** You may think it's all over anyway, so why wait around and listen to whatever they want to tell you. Besides the fact that this behavior burns bridges, you'll end up having to call HR to get answers to a lot of questions that would have been answered if you'd stayed; questions about when to expect your last check, when to expect a W-2 form, what happens to your insurance, and so on. Get it over with now so you don't have to call or come back.

- **Don't be critical of anyone.** This includes your boss, the company, your co-workers, and everyone else. Blasting people won't get you anywhere and will only ramp up the tension. Keep a professional demeanor.

- **Don't destroy any company information.** You can be prosecuted for trashing company files, deleting information from your workplace computer, or otherwise destroying company property. Leave everything intact, and don't take anything home with you that's not yours. The last thing you need is legal trouble.

- **Don't recruit employees from the company that let you go.** This is a very passive-aggressive reaction that will get you nowhere. If someone calls you at your new place of employment and asks about job opportunities, that's one thing. Trying to gut the staff of your old company is quite another.

- **Don't bad-mouth a former employer online.** By now you must know that anything you put on the Internet can live forever. So don't post nasty comments about former employers anywhere, even anonymously on job search Web sites. If your employer happens to see your comments and can guess they came from you, it can ruin your chances of getting neutral reviews when prospective employers call about you. Obviously, posting such things on your Facebook® page is nothing short of career suicide.

Once the dust has begun to settle and you finally have time to reflect, think long and hard about what went wrong with your job. Without beating yourself up or feeling inferior, try to figure out what the real problems were. Ask yourself how you might have performed better. What will you be careful *not* to do next time? Were there any early warning signals, back in the interview stage, that might have forecast this unfortunate outcome? Is this truly the right field for you? The right position? Do you still believe you're on the right career path, or would you be better off making a switch? Do your utmost to turn this into a positive learning experience.

Entrepreneurship

If you're like a lot of people, you've probably dreamed of becoming your own boss, an entrepreneur. You might imagine a life where there's no one standing over you, forcing you to follow a bunch of silly rules. No time clock to punch, no evaluations to endure, no chance of being fired. You can work when you want and stop whenever you want. You'll be free to be your own person, answering to no one.

Yes, it all sounds idyllic. But here's the unvarnished truth, from a seasoned entrepreneur: When you own your own business, you have to work much harder and longer than anyone else. Forget the "work whenever you want" idea. You need to be on the premises or at least available all the time. Every decision and every problem ends up on your plate—and you'd better make the right choices, because you have employees who depend on you for their paychecks. And while you don't have an actual "boss" to please, instead, you have multiple bosses in the form of clients or customers. And they all have their own demands, desires, and quirks. You may think you'll be escaping evaluations and getting fired, but both of these can manifest as negative reviews on Web sites like Yelp®, poor word of mouth, and customers who don't come back. It all boils down to this: *If owning your own business sounds easier and more pleasant than working for someone else, you need to think again.*

It's certainly true that some people start their own businesses, make them run, do very well, and love the whole process—and I count myself among them. However, I've learned that it takes a certain kind of person and a specific set of circumstances to make it work. So before you decide to chuck your job and go out on your own, see if the descriptions below fit you and your situation.

Who you need to be

■ *A risk taker:* You're really rolling the dice when you walk away from your job, invest your life savings, and start up a new venture without knowing if it's going to succeed. No wonder entrepreneurs always score high on the risk-taking scale! If you like to play it a little safer, but you still covet entrepreneurship, you might slowly take the reins of the family business or work your way up in an organization that you eventually take over. It's still risky, but at least you'll acquire a business that's already established.

- **Calm, steady, and focused:** Be aware that you're not going to make money—possibly *any* money—for quite a while. And the funds that do come in will be used to pay your employees, rent, utilities, and other bills and to buy product or raw materials to grow your business. So you may be living on savings for years before you start to see a profit. During this rough period, keeping a firm grasp on your goals and staying calm will be absolutely essential.

- **Disciplined and hardworking:** No one is going to tell you to get up, get going, stay late, or do the unpleasant jobs. (Hmmm, weren't those some of the great things about owning your own business that you used to dream about?) The hardest part is that you will always need to be the driving force behind everything that has to be done. And that takes discipline. If you let things slide, even a little, your business will also slide.

- **Conscientious:** Doing your work carefully, thoroughly, and well is an extension of being disciplined. If you're negligent or sloppy, it will be reflected in every area of your business, from its appearance and productivity to the attitude of your employees. So you must be meticulous and scrupulous in everything you do. Set the bar high for yourself and others will follow.

What you need to have

- **Knowledge of your business:** In my opinion, it's way too risky to start up a business that you know little or nothing about. Understanding the mechanics of the business (the equipment you need, where to buy raw materials for the best price, who your prospective clients are and how to reach them, who your competition is, and so on) and gaining experience working in the business are two essentials. Otherwise, it will be like reinventing the wheel—and who has the time and money for that?

■ *Marketing savvy:* Marketing your product or service effectively is vital to your success, although doing so is a complex and very expensive process. You can easily burn through all of your financial resources and kill your business just by choosing the wrong marketing strategies. If you aren't sure how to market what you're selling, you'll definitely need to hire an expert in the field, which will cost you plenty. But your business won't survive if your marketing strategies miss the mark.

■ *Financial backing:* Ah, yes, here's the rub! You may have a fabulous idea, a great business plan, and loads of people dying to buy your product. But if you don't have enough money to make the initial investment, hire employees, advertise, and stay afloat until your business takes off, you'll be out of the running. Taking out business loans, borrowing against the equity in your house, finding an angel investor, using an inheritance, and setting up crowdfunding are all ways that have been used to get a business up and rolling. Just be aware that you can end up losing big-time if the business goes under.

Putting it all together

Even though both of my parents were business owners, I never imagined that I would be an entrepreneur. (In fact, when I give talks on entrepreneurship, I always refer to myself as "the accidental entrepreneur"!) But looking back I can see that Jerry and I, together, had everything we needed to make SkillPath a successful company. We had the right personalities for starting a business from scratch. We already had loads of experience working in the seminar industry. We were both very hard workers who were conscientious and disciplined on the job. And we were risk takers. As you know, I left my ideal job as clinical director of Crestwood to become a professional speaker, just because it sounded more fun and exciting. Jerry gave up a career in advertising to move into the seminar industry, proving he was willing to roll the dice. And we both tended to be calm, focused types who didn't freak out when things went wrong. I don't know if we ever would have thought of starting our own seminar company if we hadn't met at work and been so professionally compatible, but once we realized we had such complementary skills and management styles, it gave us the impetus to do our own thing.

In short, we had the right stuff personally and professionally to become entrepreneurs. But here's what I think really set us apart and allowed us to succeed:

- **We had enough start-up money so we never went into debt.** I had the money from the sale of my house in California, plus quite a bit of savings accumulated over the years. (Again, thank you, Crestwood, for paying me well!) Jerry had been making a good salary at National for quite a while, and as part of his exit deal, management bought out his shares in the company. The upshot was that, between the two of us, we had enough money to start up and maintain SkillPath without ever taking out a loan. Our business was in the black from day one (although on a personal level, we lived very frugally and didn't take salaries for over a year).

- **We had a great deal of experience in all aspects of the seminar business.** I had been National's highest-rated trainer on both communications and women's topics; spent months on the road presenting; and been vice president of faculty, curricula, and publications. I had hired and trained speakers, supervised several departments, and written almost every kind of material the company needed, including the seminars themselves and the advertising copy. (Back at Crestwood, not only did I train all the staff and supervise the clinical aspects of 18 psychiatric hospitals, but I had also written the corporate newsletter and most of the business proposals and marketing pieces.) Jerry was a marketing whiz who, after leaving a five-year advertising career, had worked in the seminar business for 10 years, had served as National's president, and had developed and written countless seminars and marketing materials. Perhaps most importantly, he also knew direct mail marketing backward and forward.

■ **We had a thorough understanding of how to market our company.** Because Jerry had so much experience in marketing seminars, he was able to get the word out about SkillPath without burning through our financial resources. When we started up, we had to rent (at great cost) mailing lists of potential seminar attendees from sources like *Time*, *Newsweek*, and various business-related journals. These lists are the lifeblood of the training industry, and they represent a hefty initial expense to a start-up seminar company. Over time, we would gradually build our own in-house lists from the names of people who attended our seminars and purchased our publications, plus those who contacted us for information. But in the beginning, we depended on these pricey, rented lists. Fortunately, because Jerry already knew which lists worked best for seminar companies, we were able to zero in on the ones that gave us the most bang for our buck, so we didn't waste our money on those that didn't produce customers (a common and expensive mistake). It's the kind of thing we never would have known without having had experience in the marketing end of our business.

Am I making entrepreneurship sound impossible? It's not, but it *is* challenging. You'll work a lot harder than you would in any hired position. You'll be connected to your business 24/7, even if you're on vacation—and vacations will be short and rare. And to make it work, you *will* need to have a lot of things come together at the right time and in the right way. Whenever I give talks about founding SkillPath or on entrepreneurship in general, I always give a respectful nod to *sheer luck*.

However, if you make it, there are some wonderful benefits. You sort of become the leader of your own country. You decide how your world is going to be—every single rule comes from you. You get to say things like, "There's no dress code" or "No regular staff meetings!" You also get to think up and try new business concepts like, "Let's create a subdivision called 'CompuMaster'" or "Let's do seminars in the U.K." or "Let's try marketing a seminar on the radio." (By the way, in case you're thinking of starting a seminar company, that last idea doesn't work!)

You also get to create the kind of world for your employees that you would like for yourself. At SkillPath, we had costume contests, food contests, art contests, and dance contests. We hosted summer riverboat cruises, fall hayrides, and Valentine's Day retro sock hops at a local high school gymnasium. We had our own bowling league and our own softball team, the SkillSox! (And I might add that we were pretty darn good.) And we marched with a SkillPath banner in Kansas City's annual PrideFest. We called ourselves a "SkillPath family," and we meant it.

Finally, there is the thrill of success. Your business is your baby, and if it's successful, you're a winner. You wake up every day feeling proud of what you've accomplished, and you realize that you've become the master of your own destiny. In truth, I can think of nothing else that is quite so exhilarating!

Forging Ahead

It's inevitable. During the course of your career, situations will alter; doors will open and close; opportunities will beckon; and your dreams, goals, and aspirations will probably change—maybe even radically. Most likely you will work in several positions, several companies, and perhaps even several professions as bigger and better opportunities arise, your position is combined with another, new management brings in their own people, the job just isn't a good fit for you anymore, or you're simply ready for a new adventure. You may even decide to go into business for yourself. Whatever the reason, it's almost certain that, from time to time, you'll transition to a new position or career.

The most important piece of advice I can give is to view every transition as a positive event. It's a chance to try something new, grow, change, gain different experience, and maybe even find the perfect place to take root and flourish. If leaving your job and finding another one *isn't* your idea, remember my favorite maxim from way back at the beginning of this book: *Sometimes you can't tell the bad news from the good, especially when you're stuck in the middle of it.* Being "released" from your old job might be the best thing that could possibly happen to you, and you won't know it until you get out there and see what's next. And if you're headed for what seems to be a golden opportunity, go after it and give it everything you've got! This new position may be exactly what you've been working toward. But no matter what your circumstances, it's vitally important that you muster all the passion and positivity you can and channel it into your new life. The future awaits you: Make it a bright one!

AFTERWORD

So there you have it—you now know enough to go out into the working world and thrive! There's plenty more to learn, of course, but experience will teach you most of these lessons. In the meantime, you know how to set reasonable goals, market yourself effectively, stand out in a crowd, fit in with co-workers, and communicate effectively with just about anyone, no matter how elevated (or humble) her position. You know how to become a presence in meetings; develop a strong, productive relationship with your boss; and manage others effectively. You know how to assess your current situation objectively and—if necessary—move on to greener pastures. And you know how important it is to simply *practice kindness* in all your endeavors. In short, you're primed to get moving and get ahead—and you know you can do it!

My last bit of advice to you is this: If you pursue your goals with every ounce of positivity and passion you have, you *will* be able to find your way, no matter how many problems you face or how dire your circumstances. This is true even if you aren't a naturally positive and passionate person, for these two characteristics can be learned and acquired. Focus on the affirmative, celebrate the good, and don't let anyone or anything stand in your way.

So off you go! And as you embark on your exciting new journey, these are my hopes for you: That you find happiness in your decisions ... that you stay strong through your trials ... that you remain eager and determined to seek success in each and every day ... and that you are blessed with enough positivity and passion to see you through your entire life.

You truly are the architect of your own destiny and the master of your own fate. Seize that power and use it!

DENISE M. DUDLEY, PHD

Denise Dudley is a professional trainer, keynote speaker, author, and business consultant. She's also the founder and former CEO of SkillPath Seminars, the largest public training company in the world, which provides 18,000 seminars per year and has trained more than 12 million people in the U.S., Canada, South Africa, Australia, New Zealand, and the U.K.

Denise holds a PhD in behavioral psychology, a hospital administrator's license, a preceptor for administrators-in-training license, and a license to provide training to medical professionals in the U.S. and Canada. She's also a certified AIDS educator, a licensed field therapist for individuals with agoraphobia, a regularly featured speaker on the campuses of many colleges and universities across the U.S., and the author of Nightingale-Conant's best-selling audio series, *Making Relationships Last*. Denise speaks all over the world on a variety of topics, including management and supervisory skills, leadership, assertiveness, communication, business writing, personal relationships, and career readiness.